persona non grata

ALSO BY TOM FLANAGAN

*Winning Power: Canadian Campaigning in the Twenty-first Century*

*Beyond the Indian Act: Restoring Aboriginal Property Rights*

*Harper's Team: Behind the Scenes in the Conservative Rise to Power*

*Self-Determination: The Other Path for Native Americans*

*An Introduction to Government and Politics*

*First Nations? Second Thoughts*

*Waiting for the Wave: The Reform Party and Preston Manning*

*Metis Lands in Manitoba*

*The Collected Writings of Louis Riel*

*Riel and the Rebellion: 1885 Reconsidered*

*Louis "David" Riel: "Prophet of the New World"*

*The Diaries of Louis Riel*

*Louis Riel: Poésies de Jeunesse*

# persona non grata

▼

### THE
### DEATH OF
### FREE SPEECH
### IN THE
### INTERNET AGE

▲

TOM FLANAGAN

SIGNAL
MCCLELLAND & STEWART

Signal is an imprint of McClelland & Stewart,
a division of Random House of Canada Limited,
a Penguin Random House Company

Library and Archives of Canada Cataloguing in Publication
is available upon request.

SIGNAL ISBN: 978-0-7710-3053-6

Typeset in Dante
Printed and bound in USA

McClelland & Stewart,
a division of Random House of Canada Limited,
a Penguin Random House Company
One Toronto Street
Suite 300
Toronto, Ontario
M5C 2V6

1  2  3  4  5      18  17  16  15  14

*Then I went down to the potter's house, and there he was, making something at the wheel. And the vessel that he made of clay was marred in the hand of the potter; so he made it again into another vessel, as it seemed good to the potter to make.*

– Jeremiah 18:3–4 (New King James Version)

# CONTENTS

# INTRODUCTION

IN 2000, AMERICAN WRITER PHILIP ROTH PUB-
LISHED *THE HUMAN STAIN*, A NOVEL THAT DEALT
with, among other things, academic life in the age of political
correctness. *The Human Stain* won many prizes, became a best-
seller, and was turned into a Hollywood movie of the same
title starring Anthony Hopkins and Nicole Kidman.

The protagonist, Dr. Coleman Silk, is an aging classics professor at Athena College, a fictional institution in the Berkshire
Mountains of western Massachusetts. Silk has recently retired
after long years as the dean of arts, in which he made many
enemies by ceaseless attempts to upgrade the college's standards. Now he has returned to teaching. In one of his classes,
he regularly takes attendance to help him learn the students'
names. After several weeks, he notices that two students have
never been checked off, so he asks the others in the class,
"Does anyone know these people? Do they exist or are they
spooks?" Both absent students happen to be African American,

so they complain to the university authorities about the alleged racial slur. Then comes an academic mobbing, in which staff members whom Dr. Silk had hired and befriended turn against him while a weak president does nothing to defend him. An inquiry is set up, Dr. Silk retires, his wife dies from stress – and then things start to get really interesting, but you'll have to read the book or see the movie to find out more about this sprawling and engrossing story.

*The Human Stain* is based on real events. Roth's friend Melvin Tumin, a well-known sociologist teaching at Princeton, used exactly those words when calling the roll in class and was subjected to an inquiry for similar allegations of racism. He was exonerated, but the very fact that he could be subjected to an inquiry is sinister enough. And stupid as well, like the case of the Washington, D.C., city staffer who was fired for using the word *niggardly* (fortunately this man was quickly rehired after the mayor consulted a dictionary).

Academic mobbing is now recognized as a subspecies of workplace mobbing, and a lot has been written about both. What happened to me in late February and early March 2013, in what I call the "Incident," was something similar but also different. Colleagues at the University of Calgary didn't try to take me down; indeed, they were quite supportive, except at the highest level of the administration. Rather, I was assaulted by multiple political organizations and media outlets outside the university. It was a "virtual mobbing," in which almost everything happened online. No one grabbed me and snarled, "Up against the wall, motherf—er." No one put a dunce cap on my head, Cultural Revolution–style, and forced me to sit on a stool in front of jeering students. No one shouted at me or picketed my office. Hardly anyone spoke to me at all. Everything happened through email, websites, and social media (death by Twitter), leading to subsequent coverage in newspapers and on television.

Human beings are social animals, so shunning, ostracism, and exile are cruel tactics, even when they're not completely successful, as they weren't in my case. Remember that Socrates was given a choice between exile and drinking poison. He drank the hemlock because he thought being sent away from friends and community was a worse fate than death. Those who engage so enthusiastically in virtual mobbing should stop to think that their actions are not that different from those of a lynch mob.

Not only was the mobbing virtual, it was virtually instantaneous. All the most important events occurred in the two and a half hours it took for me to drive from Lethbridge to Calgary on the morning of February 28, 2013. In that short period, while I didn't even know what was going on, I was denounced in extravagant language by leading politicians and fired from my position as commentator by the Canadian Broadcasting Corporation (CBC). Contracts were broken and speaking invitations were withdrawn. Media outlets everywhere in the country posted inflammatory stories on their websites, based on the completely false tagline of a single YouTube posting: "Tom Flanagan okay with child pornography."

In Franz Kafka's novella *Metamorphosis,* Gregor Samsa wakes up one morning to find that he has been transformed into a cockroach-like species of vermin. Something similar happened to me. I left Lethbridge as a respected academic and public commentator and arrived in Calgary as *persona non grata*.

Virtual mobbing operates by attacking one's reputation, and with it the financial opportunities that come with reputation – consulting contracts, speaking invitations, media appearances, publishing offers. Although not directly physical, it can have medical repercussions, and having been through my own mobbing, I can see how my health could have been affected. Fortunately for me, I got through it with the support of family and old friends – and a lot of new friends too, people I hadn't known before but who care about free speech and fair play. Going through an experience like this makes you understand the importance of other people. The Beatles were right about getting by with help from your friends. And Blanche DuBois was right too; I also depended on the kindness of strangers.

I've written this book because what happened to me illustrates important tendencies in contemporary Canada threatening freedom of speech and discussion. The Incident was a perfect storm. The backdrop was a moral panic over child pornography, traceable to the hysteria of the 1980s over the phantasms of repressed memory syndrome, satanic cults in childcare centres, and pedophile rings. This particular moral panic, though started by radical feminists as part of their crusade against male power, was appropriated by conservatives, who have now created their own version of political correctness around the issue of child pornography. Those on the right don't want anyone to ask whether sentences for possession of child pornography are getting too harsh, whether too many people who are not a direct threat to others are being sent to jail. I have spent decades challenging the political correctness of leftist ideologues, who don't want anyone to ask whether the nuclear family is more than a lifestyle choice, or whether those on welfare bear some responsibility for their condition, or whether Aboriginal peoples have to adopt Canadian norms of behaviour if they hope to share the Canadian standard of living. Ironically, I now found myself shouted down by the ideologues of the right, who proved to be just as intolerant of other opinions as the ideologues of the left.

The term *political correctness* became common in the 1990s when conservatives, first in the United States and then in other countries, started using it to satirize the extremes of left-wing identity politics. At the simplest level, political correctness is a craze for politeness, a mania for euphemisms, a sort of belief in word magic, a desire to believe that renaming something will change the reality. In my own lifetime, the polite word for a person of African ancestry living in North America has gone from *Coloured* to *Negro* to *Black* to *African American* or *African Canadian*, yet the racial divide has not disappeared. *Indians* have become *Native Americans* in the United States and *First Nations* in Canada, yet their social and political problems are as severe as ever. *Illegitimate* is now a taboo word, even though more and more children are being born without the benefit of legally married parents.

But more is involved than simply too much trust in the power of euphemisms. Politically correct language is almost always adopted with an eye toward entrenching unexamined premises as part of the conventional wisdom. Take the politically correct terms *Native Americans* and *First Nations*. Both expressions imply that there is something special about being first, that the *First Peoples* (to use another expression) of the Americas should have special rights. But the chronological principle is hard to defend, and in fact we generally don't follow it. The same people who advocate special status for American Indians because they were here first would be horrified at discrimination against recent immigrants because they have arrived later. Insisting on politically correct terminology is a way of preventing anyone from asking whether chronological priority should lead to special legal status.

Another example of prohibiting questions appears in the replacement of *sex* by *gender*. Until the 1970s, men and women were known as the two sexes. If someone constructing a questionnaire wanted to know whether you were male or female, he or she would include a question labelled *Sex*. *Gender*, in contrast, was a grammatical concept encountered only in the study of foreign languages. In German, why was *die Butter* ("butter") feminine, *der Teller* ("plate") masculine, and *das Messer* ("knife") neuter, even though all three nouns had the same ending in -*er*? No one had a good answer, but you had to memorize the gender if you wanted speak correct German. In English, feminists started to substitute *gender* for *sex* in order to smuggle in their theory that sex differences – sorry, gender differences – were socially constructed. Sex was so obviously biological that it had to be banned from the discussion. Today, people "have sex" when they perform sexual intercourse, but they belong to a gender, not a sex, when they are spoken of as a member of a group.

In 2005, world-famous economist Lawrence Summers lost his job as president of Harvard University because he forgot that prohibition of questions is the first axiom of political correctness. When trying to explain why there are fewer women than men in many natural science disciplines, he proposed, as one cause among many, the well-known and uncontested fact that the normal distribution of abilities has a larger standard deviation for men than for women. That is, men are more variable than women in many different respects. With respect to intelligence, this means there are more developmentally challenged boys than girls but also more cases of high-level genius among men than women. Since succeeding in fields such as physics and chemistry requires unusual levels of intelligence, especially mathematical ability, it follows that the talent pool will be larger among men than among women; the greater male variability means there will be more men than women located at the far-right end of the normal distribution. This was not a new idea when Summers dared to speak about it; indeed, it had been popularized in *Scientific American* by Canadian psychologist Doreen Kimura, who had spent decades of meticulous research documenting the differences between men and women. But feminist activists did not want to hear that natural differences between men and women might lead to self-selection in the choice of careers.

Like Lawrence Summers, I got into trouble for asking a prohibited question. That makes me feel as if I'm in pretty distinguished, albeit undeserved, company. Summers had two uncles who won the Nobel Prize for Economics, Paul Samuelson and Kenneth Arrow. As chief economist at the World Bank, secretary of the treasury for Bill Clinton, president of Harvard, and director of the National Economic Council for Barack Obama, he is one of the most important people in the world. If Larry Summers can be brought low for violating political correctness, it can happen to anyone.

Summers is a Democrat in American politics, liberal in a moderate, technocratic way. He got into trouble for violating the political correctness of liberalism, which stipulates that natural differences between men and women are unimportant in determining professional success. I am a Conservative in Canadian politics, ideologically conservative in what I like to think of as a moderate way (though detractors like to call me extreme). I got in trouble for violating the political correctness of conservatism, which holds that anyone who looks at images of child pornography is a dangerous pervert who must be imprisoned for a substantial term. If Summers had challenged the political correctness of the right, or if I had challenged the orthodoxy of the left, probably nothing in particular would have happened. That would have been playing to type. But saying the unexpected caused us both to be deserted by people who usually would have been our friends.

Political correctness is an important theme here but not the only one. The Incident also illustrates media trends that are driven more by technology than ideology, including the hyper-acceleration of the news cycle and the impact of social media. The extreme speed-up in reporting the news, combined with the replacement of professional standards by a mob mentality, threatens rational discussion on all fronts. You can't have an intelligent conversation if there is no time for anything except demagogic slogans.

Democracy, I believe, is the best form of government that has yet to be invented. No one has improved on Abraham Lincoln's famous definition of popular government as government "of the people, by the people, and for the people." But if popular government is going to be effective, people have to be allowed to hear about the policy alternatives from among which they can choose. Shouting down speakers who offend the political correctness of the left or the right makes it harder for citizens to appreciate the choices they have to make, as well as the effects of choices they have made in the past. We all lose when rational discussion becomes impossible.

I was just one person caught in the cat's cradle of moral panic, political correctness, and thoughtless news reporting. Although I suffered some reverses, support from friends will allow my life to go on more or less as it has in the past. But the stakes surrounding child pornography are much, much higher, both for the child victims of sexual abuse and for those who are facing long prison sentences over accusations of viewing child pornography. Because its effects are so drastic, criminal law should be the last resort of a free society in dealing with social problems. Because people's lives are at stake, the resort to criminal law ought to be based on full discussion of options and examination of evidence. We need to get it right if we are going to protect our children without heedlessly creating a new class of victims. We won't get it right unless we are able to talk about it openly, without shouting down dissenting voices.

## CHAPTER 1

# COURTING CONTROVERSY

## Academic Pursuits and Public Affairs

I LIKE TO SAY THAT I'M THE ONLY PERSON WHO has ever lived in both Ottawa, Illinois, and Ottawa, Ontario. I'll keep saying it until someone stands up with evidence to contradict me.

Ottawa, Illinois, is a small industrial town in the northern part of the state. My friends' fathers worked in the sand pits or glass factory and belonged to the United Automobile Workers; their mothers were mainly homemakers. I got my first union card at sixteen when I took a part-time job at the A&P grocery store and had to join the Retail Clerks International Association. I've carried a union card ever since, for the last forty-five years as a member of The University of Calgary Faculty Association. I don't agree with all the privileges that legislators have granted to unions, but I think people working for large organizations benefit from having another organization to represent their interests.

The Flanagans were not, however, a union family; Marxists would have called us petit bourgeois. My father never had a wage or salary, but he made a good living selling auto parts on commission. Late in life, he became chairman of the local hospital board and spearheaded construction of a new building. My mother was a schoolteacher, but, as was common at the time, she retired from work to raise my sister and me. My sister became a nurse and married an accountant.

We were Roman Catholics, so I attended St. Columba parochial school and Marquette High School. I was valedictorian of my (small) high school class, and I had good SAT scores. My father wanted me to apply to Harvard, but I was fixated on the University of Notre Dame in South Bend, Indiana, whose appeal to a Midwestern Catholic boy was overwhelming. So I went there, with the help of a scholarship from the Retail Clerks International Association. It was only $500 a year, which doesn't sound like much today; yet tuition at Notre Dame was only $900 a year in 1961, when I was admitted. Tuition and fees at Notre Dame have been announced as $44,605 for the year 2013–14. That's an eightfold increase in real terms, even after adjusting for inflation. Is the education eight times better now? I sincerely doubt it.

I thought I might major in mathematics, until I went through first-year honours calculus. Although I got an A in the course, I met for the first time students with mathematical gifts that were on an altogether different level from mine. I decided I didn't want to spend my life being second-rate in my chosen career, so I tried a couple of other majors and ended up in political science. I was drawn into it by a course in political philosophy, in which we read Aristotle's *Nicomachean Ethics,* St. Augustine's *City of God,* and Hobbes's *Leviathan.* That gives you a good idea of my intellectual interests at the time. Like many young students looking for truth, I fell in love with political philosophy. I particularly came under the spell of Eric Voegelin after reading *The New Science of Politics.* It's far too complicated to explain here, but Voegelin was a scholar in the great German tradition, like a combination of G. W. F. Hegel and Max Weber.

My favourite professor at Notre Dame, Gerhart Niemeyer, recommended I go to Duke University in North Carolina to study for my Ph.D. because a former student of his, John Hallowell, taught political philosophy there. Hallowell became my supervisor, and I continued down my Voegelinian path in political theory; but I also met Allan Kornberg, newly arrived at Duke. Kornberg was originally from Winnipeg, had played nose guard for the Blue Bombers, and had wrestled professionally as the "Kosher Krusher." He had earned his Ph.D. at the University of Michigan, the leading centre of voting studies in the United States. His class on political parties, in which we had to do a computer-based piece of research, made me interested in empirical political science. Along with my friend and carrel-mate Barry Cooper, later my colleague at the University of Calgary, I also took two courses in statistics from the mathematics department – just cookbook statistics, not the real stuff derived with calculus – but by the standards of the mid-1960s, it was pretty good statistical training for a political scientist.

Political philosophy and statistics seemed like an odd combination at the time, when wars were still raging in political science between behaviouralists and traditionalists. However, I found them compatible because both approaches seek generalizations, philosophy deductively and statistics inductively. That probably says something about me. My mind naturally tends to focus not on people as individual persons but as representatives of types, placeholders in impersonal trends. Maybe that's why I often get caught up in controversies; I probably pay too much attention to abstract ideas, not enough to real people.

In 1967–68, I had the opportunity to go to West Berlin for a year to work on my dissertation and improve my rather basic knowledge of the German language. The Duke political science department had an exchange fellowship with the political science institute of the Free University of Berlin. This was still the Berlin of the Wall, Checkpoint Charlie, and the Cold War. West Berlin was swarming with so-called libertarian Marxists, while East Berlin, which I often visited, was under the thumb of real Marxists. It took many years for me to assimilate all the contradictory experiences I underwent while studying in Berlin and visiting Leipzig and Prague.

Meanwhile I had to get on with life and find a job so I could support my wife and infant son. It was a different world then. If you were a Ph.D. student from a prestigious university such as Duke, you didn't actually apply for jobs, you just told your professors you needed a job and then waited for offers to come through the mail. The first offer I received was for a one-year sabbatical replacement at the University of Texas. That was a great opportunity, but with a young family to support, I wanted more certainty than a one-year appointment. Then I got a tenure-track offer from the political science department at the University of Calgary. I had never heard of Calgary – had never been west of the Mississippi – so I had to go to the reference room of the Free University library to check out an atlas. When I finally located Calgary on the map, I said to myself, "Hey, Rocky Mountains, why not?" I later got a similar offer from McMaster University in Hamilton, Ontario; and my wife, who was from New England, wanted me to kiss off Calgary and go to McMaster so she could be closer to her relatives. I said I had already given my word to Calgary and had to follow through. I was only twenty-four, and I didn't know yet that academics don't have a higher standard for keeping promises than do other people. But I've never regretted coming to Calgary. I think growing up with a new university in a rapidly expanding city gave me unique opportunities as a researcher and writer and as a participant in public affairs.

My experience in coming to Calgary shows much the world has changed since 1968. I drove west from North Carolina, arriving at the border crossing at Coutts, Alberta, bearing no documentation except an American passport and a letter of appointment from the University of Calgary. The friendly Canadian border guard waved me through, saying I could take care of all the paperwork and get a medical exam after arriving in Calgary. Today the tac team would be called in to take down this crazy kid arriving without immigration papers.

I was hired to teach political philosophy and statistical methodology, neither of which have any particular Canadian content. But once it became clear that I would be staying in Calgary, I started reading as much as I could about Canadian history and politics. That's how I discovered Louis Riel, whom I had never heard of before crossing the border. The typical view at the time, enshrined in George Stanley's biography *Louis Riel,* was that Riel was a gifted political leader with an unfortunate streak of insanity that had expressed itself in religious monomania. But coming from outside, and not knowing anything about the constitutional and linguistic battles that had swirled around Riel, I saw him in a completely different framework – as a prophetic and millenarian religious leader. This harkened back to a book I had read as an undergraduate studying with Gerhart Niemeyer – *The Pursuit of the Millennium* by British historian Norman Cohn. Riel looked to me like a medieval prophet of the Last Days who had somehow landed in nineteenth-century Canada.

My dissertation had proven to be a dead end, so in the early 1970s I switched my research focus to Louis Riel. I spent a lot of time improving my reading knowledge of French (I never did learn to speak it) and set off across Canada and the United States looking for Riel manuscripts. I was helped enormously by Gilles Martel, a sociology professor from the Université de Sherbrooke, who had come to the same insight about Riel several years earlier and was far ahead of me in locating sources. We decided to pool our efforts, which eventually led to editing and publishing all of

Riel's manuscripts in *The Collected Writings of/Les Ecrits complets de Louis Riel* in 1985 – a centennial commemoration of the North-West Rebellion of 1885.

Martel and I had similar views of Riel, though he published in French and I in English. I think that together we revolutionized the understanding of Canada's best-known and yet most enigmatic historical figure. My book *Louis 'David' Riel: Prophet of the New World* was well received and even won best Canadian biography of 1982. Readers found it a bit perplexing that I had sidestepped the old, sterile debates about whether Riel was a traitor or a hero, and whether he was "really" insane. I depicted him rather as a Métis Joseph Smith, claiming to be divinely inspired and founding a new version of Christianity. It was provocative, but not controversial, because I wasn't taking sides for or against Riel and the Métis.

I started to become controversial shortly thereafter because, as part of my editorial work for *The Collected Writings*, I had to review the history of the North-West Rebellion. Study of the sources, including some newly discovered manuscripts, convinced me that the Canadian government had in fact dealt fairly with Métis land grievances, that Riel had provoked the rebellion for his own reasons, and that his treason trial had been fairly conducted by the standards of the day. When I published these findings in numerous articles and in the book *Riel and the Rebellion: 1885 Reconsidered*, I became not only controversial but almost radioactive in Métis circles because my interpretation undermined the mythology they had constructed in support of their contemporary land claims.

As a result of this research, the federal Department of Justice hired me in 1986 as a historical consultant and expert witness in the *Manitoba Métis Federation* case, which had already been percolating since 1976. I hadn't made a detailed study of the Manitoba claims, but the department was willing to pay me to do the research. The Crown has a lot of problems finding expert witnesses in Aboriginal cases because most of the historians and anthropologists who work in this field consider themselves part of the Aboriginal political movement and won't testify for the Crown. I, at least, was willing. Most of my research findings appeared in my 1991 book *Metis Lands in Manitoba*, which won best book of the year on Manitoba history from the Historical Society of Manitoba. I loved consulting with Crown lawyers and getting the academic recognition symbolized by the prize, but it made me even more unpopular among Métis political leaders.

This case became the Canadian equivalent of *Jarndyce v. Jarndyce*, immortalized in Charles Dickens's novel *Bleak House*. It didn't come to trial until spring 2006 and wasn't finally decided by the Supreme Court of Canada until 2013. Even then, the Supreme Court's "declaratory judgment" didn't really settle anything; it just provided talking points for future negotiations, if indeed such negotiations ever take place.

My involvement in *Manitoba Métis* led to additional expert-witness work. First, the federal Department of Justice asked me to write a report on the early history of the Lubicon Lake dispute. The case never came to trial, but my work led to several articles demystifying some of the Lubicons' claims. Then I appeared in two high-profile Indian cases, one for Treaty Six and one for Treaty Eight. As with *Manitoba Métis,* I hadn't previously done original research on these specific topics, but the Crown was willing to pay me to do the necessary work.

All these projects as a consultant on Indian land-claims litigation made me a lot of new enemies. They also drove me toward a deeper examination of questions about Aboriginal rights, expressed in my 2000 book *First Nations? Second Thoughts,* a heat-seeking missile aimed at the emerging orthodoxy that Indians were sovereign "First Nations" capable of dealing with Canada on a nation-to-nation basis. *First Nations? Second Thoughts* became a best-seller by academic standards and won two prizes, including the $25,000 Canadian Donner Prize for the year's best book on public policy (I quickly used the money to buy a new Buick because friends kept approaching me with semi-jocular ideas on how I could spend the money to their advantage). More controversy, more acclaim, more prizes . . . and more enemies.

My final foray into this field was *Beyond the Indian Act,* published in 2010 and written in collaboration with Chris Alcantara, a former M.A. student of mine; Manny Jules, the chief of the First Nations Tax Commission; and André Le Dressay, a consulting economist who has done a great deal of work for the commission. The book was a proposal for introducing private property rights onto First Nations land on a voluntary basis, meaning that no one would be compelled to do anything. Fundamentally, the thinking behind the proposal came from Manny and André, while Chris and I helped to put it in an academic envelope. The book was named one of five finalists for the Donner Prize, but it did not emerge as the winner. Of course, it made new enemies, especially Ryerson University law professor Pamela Palmater, the Idle No More diva.

Idle No More was a loosely organized Aboriginal movement that sprang up in fall 2012 in response to legislative initiatives of the Conservative government, including some minor amendments to the Indian Act. The odd name "Idle No More" originated in a teach-in held in Saskatoon to protest the Harper government's legislation. Cynics called it "Idle Some More" because its views, if ever implemented, would have the effect of erasing economic opportunities for Aboriginal peoples and thus increasing the already much too high level of Aboriginal unemployment. More of a social media network than an organized movement, Idle No More became a brand or label for the more radical Aboriginal activists to use when making their claims. I have described it here because Aboriginal activists brandishing the Idle No More label initiated the Incident that caused me so much grief.

By and large, I enjoyed my thirty years of controversy over Métis and First Nations. They had more media and political support, but my work had academic heft. All my research had been published in university presses and refereed scholarly journals. I wasn't sure that I was right about everything, or even anything; no one can ever have such certainty in the complex realm of public affairs. I saw myself, in the spirit of John Stuart Mill, as serving the public interest, challenging conventional wisdom by putting forward contrary arguments:

He who knows only his own side of the case knows little of that. His reasons may be good, and no one may have been able to refute them. But if he is equally unable to refute the reasons on the opposite side, if he does not so much as know what they are, he has no ground for preferring either opinion.

But it seems that many in native communities saw me not as an annoying or useful gadfly but as a political enemy to be destroyed if possible. That feeling was undoubtedly strengthened by the fact that I did also get drawn into politics.

## Political Hack

It took many years for my political views to mature. I grew up generally conservative, I would say. My mother never discussed politics, while my father was a Republican who voted for Kennedy in 1960 to prove that a Catholic could become president. He was at heart a Midwestern populist with a healthy mistrust of all politicians.

I thought of myself as conservative when I was at Notre Dame, but I started to drift leftward at Duke and even more so when I went to Berlin. For a few years, I saw myself as a social democrat and taught courses at the University of Calgary on Marxism and socialism. I dimly remember volunteering in one NDP provincial campaign in the early 1970s. The candidate had hemorrhoids and had to stay at home sitting on a doughnut-shaped cushion, so I helped to drop pamphlets at people's houses – not that it had any effect in Calgary.

My social-democratic phase didn't last very long, and I started drifting back to liberalism, whatever that meant. I had an opportunity to learn more about it in 1976–77 when my wife, a speech therapist working for the Calgary Board of Education, got a sabbatical to study at Gallaudet University for the deaf in Washington, D.C. I went along as "spouse of student," and one of my projects for the year was to work up a new course on liberalism. The more I read, the more I became enamoured of eighteenth- and nineteenth-century classical liberalism, especially as interpreted by Austrian economist Friedrich Hayek. I came to Washington as a confused seeker and left as a convinced Hayekian (I also watched Jimmy Carter walk down Pennsylvania Avenue on inauguration day and Sun Myung Moon deliver a speech in Korean at the Washington Monument).

Back in Canada, I started reading everything published by the Fraser Institute, which is generally animated by a Hayekian worldview, though not in the same sectarian way as some followers of the Austrian school of economics. In practical politics, I started voting for the Progressive Conservatives (PC). Though they didn't really represent Hayek's principles of free markets, restrained government, and spontaneous order, they seemed like the best available option. Actually, I had almost no interest in contemporary practical politics, as I was living mentally in the nineteenth century with my research on Louis Riel and the Métis. I welcomed Brian Mulroney's victory in 1984, thinking maybe that would mean progress toward controlling deficit spending and privatizing Crown corporations. Mulroney did deliver part of what I hoped to see, but I was disillusioned by his pandering to Quebec. Yet I voted PC again in 1988, not wanting to jeopardize the Free Trade Agreement with the United States. My wife, however, voted Reform; she's always a step ahead of me.

After 1988, I became increasingly disappointed with Mulroney and the PCs, as deficits again spiralled out of control and Canada seemed headed for a constitutional crack-up over the Meech Lake Accord. At first I thought the Reform Party was just another confused populist movement, of which Alberta has seen so many; but then one of my graduate students gave me the Reform's *Blue Book*, which had been mostly written, I later found out, by Stephen Harper. I read it cover to cover and concluded that here was a party I could support with enthusiasm. I sent in a $100 cheque but didn't do anything else, though I did get to know Preston Manning in a series of brown-bag "egghead lunches" held on campus in fall 1990. No one was more surprised than I when, early in winter 1991, Preston asked me to come to work for him with the grandiose title Director of Policy, Strategy, and Communications. I should have said no. It was too much like the title Louis Riel gave himself, Prophet, Priest-King, and Infallible Pontiff.

I didn't last very long with Reform, just twenty months. I've described the whole experience in my book *Waiting for the Wave*, though my perspective on it is somewhat different now than when I wrote that book in 1993–94. Looking back, I can see that I didn't have the practical political experience necessary for the job I was supposed to do. I learned at a furious pace, but it still wasn't enough. Also, I was still thinking of the Reform Party as a vehicle for a fairly pure form of conservatism or classical liberalism, call it what you will. I wasn't mentally prepared for all the compromises necessary to build a winning political coalition. And finally, I came under the spell of Stephen Harper, who privately discussed with me his many complaints about Manning's leadership. Although Harper was sixteen years younger than I, his keen intellect, strategic insight, and broad knowledge of politics were impressive, indeed overwhelming. I thought we were in agreement that Manning's populism was leading him to jettison important free-market principles. Of course, this seems laughable from the vantage point of today, now that Harper has abandoned many of those principles and become a practitioner of supply management in the dairy industry, massive subsidies to corporations, funding of local pet projects, and deficit spending. I now understand that this was simply the beginning of Harper's drive to achieve his own leadership. He is a man of such great ability, coupled with the desire to be in control, that he can't be happy for long unless he holds the alpha position.

I resigned at the end of 1992, unfairly disillusioned with Manning's leadership but still holding to what I saw as the underlying principles of the Reform Party. That started my career as a media pundit. Reporters were eager to talk to me because I was one of very few people with academic or professional credentials who had been inside the Reform Party and was willing to talk about it. I had been in the media before because of my heretical views about Louis Riel, but those appearances were episodic and limited to a small range of subjects. Now I was in demand almost every day as reporters called to get my take on what Manning and Reform were up to. That was fine as far as it went, but talking to journalists was time-consuming and unpaid, and I could see that many reporters had a not-so-hidden agenda of using my comments to discredit Reform. I wanted to write for the media, to express my views directly and get paid for it.

The Byfield family was kind enough to let me write some columns and book reviews in *Alberta Report,* and I gradually broke into the pages of newspapers such as the *Calgary Herald.* My big break came in fall 1997, when the *Globe and Mail* invited me to write a monthly column. I was supposed to represent the view from the prairies, as part of a roster of twenty writers from across the country who would each write once a month from the vantage point of their regions. I often wrote about Reform issues but also about native claims and whatever else was happening out West. It was a great opportunity to apply my Hayekian version of conservatism/classical liberalism to the issues of the day, to broaden my reputation as a commentator on all sorts of things. Of course, every time I wrote I made new enemies because, when I wasn't poking holes in the populist delusions of Reform, I was goring the infinitely numerous sacred cows of the Canadian left.

In fall 2000, I jumped to the *National Post* because my editor at the *Globe* was starting to edit too much. My most memorable piece at the *Post* was undoubtedly the "Open Letter to Ralph Klein" of January 24, 2001, usually known as the "Firewall Letter." While I held the pen, it was a collective production of six Calgary conservatives, spearheaded by Stephen Harper. Harper was then president of the National Citizens Coalition, and the Firewall Letter was meant to be the first step in his campaign to get the better-off provinces to resist federal intrusions into their constitutional jurisdiction – all for the longer-term purpose of weakening the redistributive welfare state, much of which is built on the federal government's use of its so-called "spending power" in areas of provincial jurisdiction. That campaign never went anywhere, however, because about the same time Stockwell Day fell into trouble as leader of the Canadian Alliance, and Harper decided to take a run at the leadership once the party declared there would be a campaign.

Initially, I was just one of a group of Calgary friends who came together to help Harper get started, but my involvement deepened in November 2001. The campaign team that we had recruited wasn't working out well, and Harper fired everyone, fell into one of the despondent moods that are well known to those who have worked with him, and thought seriously about quitting the race. To keep him going, I said I would manage the campaign. Easy enough to say – I'd never even worked in a campaign, let alone run one! But I quickly learned how to superintend an activity without really knowing much about it. Find good people, take their advice, and make sure they stay on schedule and within budget. Fortunately, Harper had the friends and political contacts to lead us to the people who could get the job done under my loose supervision.

Thus began a period of intense political activity lasting four years. I was at various times manager of leadership campaigns; director of operations, chief of staff, or senior political adviser to the Leader of the Opposition; manager of the 2004 national Conservative campaign; and rapid-response director in the 2005–06 national campaign. I was Harper's chief organizer, under various labels. Throughout this time I had almost nothing to do with formulating policy, and indeed I gradually gave up my old infatuation with political philosophy. Politics became for me a story about one thing – winning – and policies were merely props in the campaign script.

I did many things in these years, but my main contribution to Harper's success was to help build the fundraising machine that has fuelled the Conservatives' dominance over the last decade. Of course, I didn't do it myself; my role was to provide administrative support and protection for those actually doing the work. The first step was to build the Constituency Information Management System (CIMS) database to combine voter identification and fundraising information. The second step was to bring in the Responsive Marketing Group, headed by Michael Davis of Toronto, to provide massive telephone capacity for voter ID, Get Out the Vote, and fundraising by telephone solicitation. It was Davis who came up with the simple but brilliant idea of prospecting for money among our huge lists of identified supporters, thus continually building our donor base. The third step was to transfer overall management to Irving Gerstein (now a senator), who had been the head of PC fundraising for decades. This required some delicate transition measures while Irving learned to appreciate the innovations that had come from the Reform/Alliance side as well as from

Michael Davis's ingenuity and how to integrate everything with his own invaluable experience from the Tory side.

The result was a fundraising system that every year raises more money than all the other parties put together. And it is this money that has led to the Conservative majority government because it paid for the negative ads that undermined Liberal leaders Stéphane Dion in 2008 and Michael Ignatieff in 2011. Those elections were won before the writ was ever dropped; the writ-period campaigns were mopping-up operations. So my biggest political legacy was to become the godfather of big-money fundraising and negative advertising – how ironic is that for a Hayekian political philosopher? Hegel might have seen it as an example of the "cunning of reason," and Hayek might have called it an unintended consequence of spontaneous order.

As described in my book *Harper's Team,* I gave Harper and the Conservative Party my best efforts until June 2005, when I went back full-time to university life (though I did come back to work in the war room in the 2006–06 campaign). I had been trying to commute between Calgary and Ottawa; and not only was I getting worn down, I felt that the job of preparing for the next campaign required someone to be in Ottawa all the time. I also thought that Doug Finley, the deputy manager to whom I had already delegated extensive responsibilities, would be a better manager than I could hope to be – and that turned out to be a correct assessment. I don't think I could ever have won a national election. I'm not tough enough. You have to be a human bulldozer like Doug Finley to push your party all the way to victory. R.I.P., Doug.

I was also worn out from trying to work with Harper. He has enormous gifts of intelligence, willpower, and work ethic; but there is also a dark, almost Nixonian side to the man. He believes in playing politics right up to the edge of the rules, which inevitably means some team members will step across ethical or legal lines in their desire to win for the Boss. He can be suspicious, secretive, and vindictive, prone to sudden eruptions of white-hot rage over meaningless trivia, at others time falling into week-long depressions in which he is incapable of making decisions. I was tired of all the psychodrama, and I feared, as I still do, that he might someday bring himself down Nixon-style by pushing too hard against the network of rules constraining authority in a constitutional government. The Senate scandal of spring 2013, in which the prime minister's secretive management of a small issue turned it into a major embarrassment, was exactly the sort of thing I have long feared might happen.

Just as I had written *Waiting for the Wave* shortly after leaving the employment of the Reform Party, I now started writing *Harper's Team*. When I told Harper in person that I was writing it, he didn't object, but months later he had his chief of staff, Ian Brodie, call me to ask me not to publish it. I said, Sorry, this train has left the station, though I agreed to send the manuscript to the Prime Minister's Office for vetting before publication. That was the end of my personal relationship with Harper. The man who once said to me, "Tom, it's always dangerous to share information" couldn't get over the fact that I had published a book about the years I had worked for him. Doug Finley did try to bring me back to help prepare for the 2008 election, but that brief experiment ended abruptly when the second edition of *Harper's Team* came out. Suddenly no one was answering my emails and phone calls – a peculiarly graceless ending, I thought.

While Harper is secretive to an unusual degree, it must be pointed out in fairness that the whole Canadian political system is secretive. In the United States, it is taken for granted that every highly placed insider, such as a chief of staff or campaign manager, may eventually write a book about his years of service, but very few such books are ever published in Canada. I think Canada is poorer for it, but maybe that's just my Americanism showing through.

After the 2006 election was over and I was completely out of the Conservative organization, I resumed the pundit activities that I had suspended four years earlier when I went to work for Harper in Ottawa. I started writing a column on a monthly basis for the *Globe and Mail* because Natasha Hassan, who had always treated me well when she was comment editor at the *National Post,* had moved over there. I also freelanced quite a bit on TV until I signed an exclusive contract in 2010 with the CBC. The general idea was that I would appear twice a week as part of the "Power Panel" on Evan Solomon's daily News Network show, *Power and Politics,* and occasionally on other programs as needed.

I generally enjoyed appearing on *Power and Politics.* I find a lot of Canadian public affairs programming a bit dull, so I tried to liven things up with jokes and anecdotes, sometimes even bringing props along with me, such as a toy wooden gun to hold when we talked about the Firearms Registry. Evan and the other staff seemed to like it and kept encouraging me to do more, though I eventually ran out of ideas for props. I could always fall back on my spontaneous sense of humour, but that was also a bit dangerous because my humour is very dry, sometimes tending toward black, and people can be offended. The worst came true on November 30, 2010, when I got a foretaste of what mobbing is like.

The Power Panel would discuss almost anything in Canadian politics, usually with a couple of hours' notice as to the topics but occasionally having to react to something out of the blue. During the Power Panel on November 30, 2010, we were asked, with no time to prepare, to talk about Wikileaks leader Julian Assange, who was in the news that day. When forewarned about a topic, I would try to have something ready to say; but having nothing prepared on this subject, I fell back on black humour. I said with a laugh, "I think Assange should be assassinated, actually." President Obama "should put out a contract and maybe use a drone or something." I thought it was obvious I was joking, but when Evan replied that this was "pretty harsh stuff," I realized maybe the joke wasn't coming through. So I said, "I'm feeling very manly today, Evan," which I thought would make it apparent. But the Wikileaks people are an international cult with little sense of humour at the best of times, so a bad joke about assassinating their icon wasn't going to amuse them.

My comments unleashed an avalanche of vitriolic email and death threats from around the world. Someone put up a Facebook site with my contact information to facilitate the

swarming. I went back on Evan's show two days later to apologize, but nothing would stop the flow of abuse; I just had to
ride out the storm.

What made it worse was that left-wing activists in several
cities asked the local police to lay charges against me for incitement to murder. Lawyers told me this was a stretch. A couple
of sections of the Criminal Code could conceivably be
invoked, such as section 319, Public Incitement to Hatred, and
section 465(1)(a), Conspiracy to Commit Murder, but these
were never meant to apply to bad jokes. Yet you never know
what might happen when the judicial system is involved. For
weeks I would lay awake at night worrying that some headline-
seeking Crown attorney might decide to take a run at me.

I vowed never to joke about murder or assassination again;
it's just too serious. And as I lay there thinking about it, I got a
little taste of what it's like to be alone and friendless, afraid
that the authorities are coming after you. I've led a pretty shel-
tered live. I've never been in prison, like Conrad Black. I was
never held hostage by terrorists, like Bob Fowler. I never
courted danger by joining the army or the police. I never even
went to summer camp. Now I was getting a small virtual taste
of persecution. It made me feel some sympathy for Julian
Assange, facing prosecution in Sweden for alleged sexual
offences that strike me as borderline, based on whatever we
can know from media accounts. I have no sympathy for the
Wikileaks enterprise, which may have cost the lives of innocent people in the Middle East and elsewhere, but I could
imagine myself in the position of a hunted man, like Assange.

Ironically, I think this experience helped give me greater sympathy for the victims of criminal justice, such as men serving years in prison for doing nothing worse than looking at child pornography, never having touched an actual child. Call it my Conrad Black moment, though it hardly compares with his five years in American prisons. Criminal justice was never a special field of study for me, but I used to be reflexively in favour of law and order, like most conservatives. Now I would say my views are more nuanced, and I worry about putting too many people in jail who are no threat to anyone except themselves. So thank you, Julian Assange, and I hope you get a fair trial if it ever comes to that.

I thought I was through with party politics after the publication of *Harper's Team* sundered my links with the federal Conservatives, but I got drawn into the Wildrose Party of Alberta because of my earlier connection with Danielle Smith. I had known Danielle for about twenty years, ever since she had taken a political science course from me on statistical research methods and I had recommended her for an internship at the Fraser Institute. We had stayed in touch over the years and collaborated on a couple of small projects. Thinking the PCs could use some pressure from the right, I had voted for Wildrose and its predecessor, the Alberta Alliance, but had not been otherwise involved until Danielle decided to run for Wildrose leader in spring 2009. Then I publicly announced my support for her and the party.

After Danielle won the leadership, she asked me to advise her on party organization and then to help with long-range campaign planning. I was happy to become an unpaid adviser with no administrative responsibilities. I met periodically with a somewhat shifting group of Wildrose people throughout 2010 and early 2011, discussing all aspects of running a full-scale provincial campaign.

Danielle formalized the campaign team in late summer 2011, appointing Cliff Fryers chairman and Rick Anderson manager. I was supposed to be an assistant to Rick, taking some responsibility for operations while he concentrated on communications. I had to have a limited role because I was teaching full-time in fall 2011. We feared that a new PC leader might call a snap election, so I couldn't have then taken on the full responsibility of management. Rick, however, found that he was unable to continue, so in late November Danielle asked me to take over from him. Now I could agree to do that because it was becoming apparent that there would be no election until 2012, probably not until after the budget would be approved in March. I wasn't scheduled to teach in the coming term, so I could take leave to become the manager.

I immediately put aside all my other projects and stepped in, working without pay because at that time Wildrose seemed short of money. The team recruited under my management put on a campaign of a type never mounted before in Alberta by an opposition party. All observers agree that we lost in the end not because of the campaign but because several candidates, including the leader herself, went badly off message with spontaneous comments during the last phase of the campaign. My staff and I tried to play whack-a-mole, but there were just too many episodes to deal with. In spite of a terrible final week, the campaign elected seventeen Wildrose members and made Danielle Leader of the Official Opposition, creating a platform for an even stronger run at victory in the next election. Instead of going into debt as campaigns often do, we left the party with a surplus of $600,000, which sustained it throughout the rest of 2012 when no one else felt like raising money.

I had no complaints at the time. The party paid me a bonus after the campaign, and Danielle offered me an advisory contract to draw the lessons from the campaign and digest them for the future. At the end of 2012, I said that job was done, so she asked me to stay on to initiate long-range planning for the 2016 election campaign. At the time of the Incident, then, I had a small behind-the-scenes connection with Wildrose but was otherwise fully occupied with my career as a university professor, writer, and commentator on public affairs.

As I now look back on it, I've had a rather odd career. I never reached the highest level of achievement in any area, but I was one step away in several. I published a great deal as a scholar, my books sold well by academic standards, and I was rewarded with several Canadian prizes as well as membership in the Royal Society of Canada. Yet true eminence in the academic world means honourary degrees and international prizes, and none of those ever came my way. I wrote regularly for newspapers, especially the *Globe and Mail,* which I'm sure most academics would love to do, but I was never a marquee columnist like Jeffrey Simpson or Andrew Coyne. I appeared regularly on the CBC News Network with Evan Solomon, but the top level of recognition would be to appear on the main network with Peter Mansbridge, and I was there only occasionally. I certainly never came close to having my own show à la David Suzuki. I managed political campaigns, but I was an academic dilettante in the small world of professional campaigners, and I never won a national or provincial election as a manager. I had been an expert witness in some important litigation, but not nearly as often as, say, historical geographer A. J. Ray, who has written an interesting and important book, *Telling It to the Judge,* about his experiences.

I'm not complaining about this; I've loved every minute of my diversified career. But it was a distinctive pattern – not at the top of anything but near the top in a variety of activities. I wasn't anywhere in particular but seemed to be everywhere at once – in the university and in think tanks, in the news-papers and on television, in the backrooms of politics advising party leaders, in the courtroom fencing with lawyers. That irritated a lot of people, particularly because I was obviously having fun playing Don Quixote, tilting at the windmills of conventional wisdom and settled opinion. After all, if you're a Hayekian, you can't help but be critical of many policies in a left-leaning social democracy such as Canada.

I know I made a lot of enemies. First there were the Métis and Indian leaders whose claims I kept challenging. I saw myself as forestalling yet more raids on the public treasury, but they thought I was blocking implementation of their rights. Then there were the partisans of other parties, who blamed me for helping Stephen Harper's Conservatives come to power, as well as the ideological leftists, who were appalled by my critiques of the welfare state, human rights commissions, and other Canadian shibboleths.

And the longer I was out there playing the role of free-thinking iconoclast, the more I was cutting myself off from actual supporters. First to go were Manning and the Prestonians, who were offended by my criticism of Reform populism. Then it was Harper, who couldn't get over the book I had written about him, even though it was mostly laudatory. The Conservative Party is so centred around his leadership that lots of other people with whom I had once worked now saw me as a nuisance – irritating at best, dangerous at worst.

All the things I was doing in public also drew me away from the university. When I was younger, I had been very involved in university affairs. I was a department head for five years and served as a special assistant to two different presidents. I was on lots of boring committees, and I knew all the vice-presidents and deans by name. But most of the people I used to know have retired, and I have not been on a university-wide committee for more than twenty years. I couldn't tell you the names of more than a couple of deans and vice-presidents, let alone pick them out of a crowd (and it would be a large crowd, as university administration has expanded exponentially during the years of my career). Decision makers at the University of Calgary knew me as a virtual presence in the media, not as a real person who might need defending.

I had made myself a dangerously exposed target for mobbing. I was ready to become *persona non grata*.

## CHAPTER 2

# THE INCIDENT

### Prequel

ON NOVEMBER 6, 2009, I FLEW TO WINNIPEG TO give a lecture entitled "Campaign Ethics: Do Canadian Election Campaigns Pass the Smell Test?" I had been invited by Jared Wesley, an assistant professor in the University of Manitoba's Department of Political Science, and philosopher Arthur Schafer, a well-known ethicist. I had never met Schafer, though I knew who he was because he is frequently quoted in the Canadian media, commenting on ethical issues in public life. I knew Jared well because he had done his doctoral studies at the University of Calgary. I wasn't one of his professors, but we had often chatted about his thesis research, which dealt with political campaign platforms.

The lecture on ethics was not a scheduled class, but it was definitely an academic event, held at noon in a large university auditorium. A few days before, Laura Blakley, a reporter for the student newspaper, *The Manitoban*, emailed me to ask if she could record my lecture for a possible podcast. I agreed, as I have always done to such requests. It seems quaint now to think that anyone would ask permission to make a recording.

In my presentation, I started by discussing commonly recognized "dirty tricks": tearing down opponents' signs, planting spies in their organization, jamming their switchboard or website, and so on. Then I moved on to what I regard as the deeper issue. Campaigns are not a seminar designed to get at the truth; they are a form of persuasive speech designed to build a coalition of supporters. All campaign communications have to be seen in that context, in which truth takes a back seat to political impact. This is deeply at odds with the university's mandate of discovering and disseminating knowledge, but it reflects the nature of politics, in which there is no truth in any absolute sense. No one knows for sure what the best set of policies is. We have opinions about complicated situations, not demonstrable solutions to mathematical problems.

Since we, as fallible human beings, can't know for sure what's true in politics, we resort, in democratic societies, to the adversarial process of campaigns and elections to choose those who will make policy decisions. Winning an election is no guarantee of being "right." There will be other elections in the future if voters don't like the results of what they have voted for. It's like the judicial process, which is another adversarial exercise. We don't know for sure what justice means in any particular case. The best we can do is to set up an argumentative process in which each side can make its best case under established rules of procedure and then let a judge or jury decide. Only God can render justice; human beings have to follow the law.

I was speaking from notes without a prepared text, but here's what I said, according to Laura Blakley's recording, which was online for a while in spring 2013:

> There is the ever-present partisanship in an adversarial system. Everything that is said in politics, and I'm quite serious when I say everything, is said to promote your party and build your electoral coalition. This is, I think, actually defensible in a larger scheme of things because politics, like our system of laws, is an adversarial system. We believe, I think, that the worst scumbag, to quote General [Rick] Hillier, deserves a good defence in court. We think it is valuable to make whatever case can be made on behalf of even the least-deserving client. But we think that the process itself is valuable and that we expect lawyers to take positions in the interests of their clients, we don't expect that these are things that the lawyer necessarily believes personally.

So far, so abstract. Then I tried to make it concrete, which is an essential part of teaching. The example that jumped into my head was how Canadian Alliance leader Stockwell Day got into trouble in 2000 when he accused Red Deer lawyer Lorne Goddard of actually supporting child pornography because he was defending a client accused of possessing child pornography:

Stockwell Day got into big trouble some years ago when he couldn't draw that distinction and he accused a lawyer who had defended, I can't remember all the details, but the lawyer had defended somebody accused, I think, of child pornography and Mr. Day suggested the lawyer himself believed it was okay to have child pornography.

If I had stopped at that point, there would be no further story, but then I did something I often do in the classroom when I'm trying to explain a long, complex train of ideas: I made a sidebar comment to break up the flow and give everyone a diversion: "That actually would be another interesting debate for a seminar, like what's wrong with child pornography, in the sense they're just pictures?" Then I made a little joke to cap off the sidebar: "But I'm not here to debate that today and I don't have any exhibits here, I have to stick with the campaign process. . . ." And then I went back to the main point I was trying to make:

> The point is, we believe in a world where nobody knows the truth for sure, I guess I'm convinced of that point by John Stuart Mill, we have to rely on adversarial processes to approximate the truth as best we can.

So that's how it all started – a couple of sentences about child pornography in the midst of a seventy-five-minute session on campaign ethics. I didn't state a position; I spontaneously asked a question as a way of punctuating a rather long train of thought. I raised a question about child pornography not because I had anything particular to say about that topic but because I had just been talking about Stockwell Day's unfortunate experience, and one thing leads to another when you're speaking extemporaneously. However, it is very much worth asking why Canada has criminalized certain kinds of pictures and punishes their possession with mandatory minimum jail sentences; I'll return to that subject later in this book.

The two-word phrase *just pictures* was really the source of all the later trouble. It's a classic example of the difference between the denotation and the connotation of words. Strictly speaking, child pornography, at least in its pictorial form, is "just pictures," images on a page or screen that people look at. It is an image, not an action, though it may be an image of an action. So to call child pornography "just pictures" is denotatively correct; but the connotations are all wrong for a public statement because the words *just pictures* sound dismissive, as if child pornography is unimportant, nothing to get excited about.

I wouldn't have chosen those words if I had been trying to make a public statement about child pornography, but *just pictures* is a valid phrase to use in a classroom setting to make students start thinking about the topic. Why, indeed, do we treat a photograph or a painting or even a cartoon of a young child performing fellatio on an adult male as different from a landscape painting or a photograph of a sunset or the nude sculpture of Venus de Milo? It's a good question, to which there are lots of good answers. Using a phrase such as *just pictures* is done for shock value, to signal to students that this is an important question that requires going back to first principles to find an answer. Not that I thought about all this at the time. When I raised the question, I was more or less on autopilot. Most of the best moments in the classroom come spontaneously, so you have to let yourself go if you hope to be an effective teacher.

I can't remember that anyone in the audience was offended; they all seemed to understand what was going on (student reporter Laura Blakley later claimed to have been stunned, but she didn't mention anything to me at the time). No one pursued it during the question period, or afterwards when individuals came up to continue the discussion, or in the evening when a group of students and professors went out for dinner. Blakley made her recording and quoted me in her story in *The Manitoban*, but that didn't lead to anything further, except that unknown parties and organizations may have added the story to their opposition research files. It didn't surface again until February 27, 2013, in Lethbridge. In the meantime, though I was often in the news, I never mentioned child pornography again because it wasn't part of my research and I had no special interest in the subject.

## The Incident

On January 21, 2013, I received a speaking invitation from the Southern Alberta Council on Public Affairs (SACPA), a Lethbridge group that has been hosting speakers since 1967.

SACPA gets some money from the University of Lethbridge because it sponsors "town and gown" events, but it's basically an independent organization with a rather left-wing reputation. But that didn't bother me; I've often spoken to left-wing groups who want to be challenged. Perhaps too naively, I've always considered any group that takes ideas seriously to be a friendly audience. The invitation came by email from Lisa Lambert, a Ph.D. student in my department who was working part-time for SACPA while finishing her dissertation. We agreed on a date of February 27, and a title of "Is It Time to Reconsider the Indian Act?"

Lethbridge is about 225 kilometres south of Calgary. I drove there the afternoon of February 27, listening on my car's CD player to Sue Grafton's latest novel in her alphabet series, prophetically entitled *V is for Vengeance* (it's one of her best books, by the way). After I arrived, I had a quick dinner with the SACPA president and a few old friends from the University of Lethbridge, then went to the 7 p.m. event, which was located in a classroom on the university campus. It was not a scheduled class, but everything about the event – the invitation from a graduate student, the dinner with colleagues, the location on campus – had put me in academic mode. I should have paid more attention to an email a Lethbridge friend had sent me that morning, warning that Idle No More supporters from surrounding First Nations were planning to attend. I had forwarded the email to Lisa Lambert, and she had asked campus security to be on hand, but I wasn't too worried about it. I've spoken to native audiences before and things had remained on respectful terms, in spite of profound disagreements. But this would be very different. The room was packed with obviously hostile people, and more were standing outside the doors, unable to get in because of university fire-safety regulations.

I didn't learn until later that there had been extensive preparations beforehand. On February 25, Arnell Tailfeathers had met with other Idle No More activists on the Blood Reserve and had decided to use my presentation as an occasion for an attack on my reputation. "From what I can tell, Flanagan has been dangerous to First Nations people for however long he's been in Canada. His viewpoints, they just kind of seem to undermine treaties and the Indian Act, and everything," Tailfeathers later told the Aboriginal publication *Alberta Sweetgrass*. Via Twitter and Facebook, Tailfeathers and his friends encouraged Idle No More supporters from all reserves in the area to attend. Piikani activist Leroy Little Mustache also made plans to ask me about my Manitoba comments on child pornography. Tailfeathers told *Sweetgrass* that he made sure the batteries on his cellphone would be fully charged when Little Mustache would ask me about child pornography.

After a brief introduction, I spoke for about forty minutes on the difficulty of amending or replacing the Indian Act. Canadian public opinion about the Indian Act is dominated by right-wing and left-wing utopianisms that cancel each other out, leaving little room to build political support for major changes. The right fantasizes about getting rid of the Indian Act, of Indian reserves, and of separate legal status altogether, while the left likes to pretend that Canada's six hundred Indian bands are really sovereign nations. But even if the climate of opinion makes major changes hard to achieve, both Liberal and Conservative governments have passed numerous small amendments to the Indian Act in the last twenty-five years. I talked about some of these, and what might be on the agenda for the near future. I thought it was a restrained, practical talk about the all-too-real difficulties of getting anything done in this field. But no one cared.

As soon as I finished, it became obvious that most of the audience had not come to listen and ask questions but to denounce me. The first "questioner" announced that she was tired of being silenced and moved from the back of the room up to the speaker's area, where she made a long speech that I never did understand. A lot of it had to do with former Reform MP Myron Thompson and a Cree woman from Manitoba named Leona Freed who had become a public critic of how Indian reserves are governed. Another woman, moving in from outside the room, launched an even longer and louder harangue about how I was "pure evil" and had been making enormous amounts of money by helping the federal and provincial governments keep native people in chains. It was completely chaotic, and none of the event organizers were doing anything to restore order.

I should have gotten out of there, but I persisted, making small points and corrections when there was a question I could understand and hoping that tempers would cool down. In fact, they did, to some extent. After we'd been at it two and a half hours and the event finally ended, a number of (mostly) younger native people came up to shake hands. They gave me an Idle No More lapel pin to put on for photo ops, and we posed in front of an INM poster. A couple of them asked if I would be willing to speak again before other native audiences, maybe even debate INM icon Pamela Palmater, and I said, "Sure." One woman, a professional actress, wanted to get together for lunch so she could give me a bottle of water from the Athabasca River to drink (I had said during the Q&A that the oil sands were not making the water carcinogenic, and of course I would drink it). I went back for a glass of wine at my hotel, thinking it had been a brutal evening but that it had ended on an upbeat note. I wasn't even thinking about, and no one mentioned to me, the few seconds of dialogue that would dominate the news going forward.

In the middle of the evening, Levi Little Mustache stood up and made a long, rambling statement that was almost unintelligible to me. The only two points I understood were that he was quoting the remark about child pornography I had made at the University of Manitoba, and he was asking whether I was really the father of the IKEA monkey. The latter question stemmed from a recent appearance on Evan Solomon's *Power and Politics*, on which I had worn my most prized possession – a winter coat made from a buffalo robe. The enormous coat caused a lot of hilarity, including questions about whether I was related to Darwin, the IKEA monkey, a baby Japanese macaque who was found wandering in the parking lot of an IKEA store in Toronto in a shearling coat. Politicians, of course, pride themselves on evading all questions, but the culture of the university is to try to give an answer, even when you're not quite sure what the question is. I quickly admitted to being Darwin's father, then tried to answer the question about my Manitoba remarks.

My career has been littered with errors. My approach has always been to plunge in, take risks, do the job, and clean up mistakes later. But this is one mistake I shouldn't have made – and wouldn't have made if I had been thinking politically rather than academically. I knew I had said something about child pornography in Manitoba a few years ago, but on the spur of the moment I couldn't remember exactly what I had said or what the context was. Nonetheless, I plunged in:

> On the child pornography issue, since that was brought up, you know, a lot of people on my side of the spectrum, on the conservative side of the spectrum, are on a jihad against, ah, pornography and child pornography in particular, and I certainly have no sympathy for child molesters, but I do have some grave doubts about putting people in jail because of their taste in pictures. I don't look at these pictures, but . . . the closest I ever came to it was at one point in my career, it's a long story, I got put on the mailing list of the National [sic] Man/Boy Love Association and I started getting their mailings for a couple of years so that's about the closest I ever came to child pornography, so, you know, it is a real issue of personal liberty to what extent we put people in jail for doing something in which they do not harm another person. . . .

At that point, there were so many boos and catcalls that I just gave up trying to explain what I meant, and we went back to discussing the Indian Act. To most people in the room, it would have been nothing but a bizarre interlude in a bizarre evening, except that Arnell Tailfeathers recorded everything with a cellphone camera and put up the excerpt overnight on YouTube with the tagline "Tom Flanagan okay with child pornography." Tailfeathers even recorded himself saying, "Gotcha, Tom," in the middle of my answer, showing that entrapment had been the point of asking the question in the first place. Yet no one mentioned it again during the Q&A or afterwards, and I went to bed that night not even thinking about it.

In light of the subsequent media brouhaha, it's important to be clear about what I did and didn't say. I didn't say that I'm okay with child pornography, or that it is a victimless crime, or that it doesn't harm anyone. I didn't actually make a statement at all. I simply said that I had questions and doubts about the necessity of putting people in jail if their only offence was to look at child pornography and they themselves hadn't harmed another person. In other words, could we consider something like the law in Great Britain, which does not prescribe a mandatory minimum jail sentence for simple possession or viewing of child pornography, at least for a first offence?

The word *harm* has drawn a lot of attention, so it is important to understand what I was getting at. I always use it in the context of the famous essay *On Liberty*, where John Stuart Mill distinguished between "harm" (an assault on the person, property, or rights of another person) and "contingent damage" (unintended and indirect effects). I didn't get a chance to explain that in Lethbridge, but I'll go into it in detail in a later chapter on child pornography.

In passing, let me clarify my comment about the North American Man/Boy Love Association (NAMBLA). When I was working for the Reform Party of Canada in 1992, the party was embarrassed by several neo-Nazis from the Heritage Front who had joined a constituency association in Toronto. In response, the party assigned me to look for any other racists or neo-Nazis who might have joined the party, so they could be expelled. As part of my research, I took out a subscription to the Heritage Front periodical *Up Front* to see what names might pop up there. I should have used a false name and post office box for the subscription, but I was new to politics then and it didn't occur to me.

A few years later the Heritage Front disbanded and stopped publishing its magazine, and then without warning I started getting newsletters from neo-Nazi organizations all over the United States and Great Britain. At the same time I also started receiving the NAMBLA Bulletin. I didn't respond to any of these mailings, and they all eventually ceased. I have always assumed, though I have no hard evidence, that the Heritage Front must have sold its mailing list to a broker, or maybe someone gave my name to NAMBLA as a sick joke. Anyway, I've told the story before to audiences because I think it's funny: you start out with instructions to look for racists and you end up on a pedophile mailing list. I thought telling the story that night might ease some of the tension in the room, but the Lethbridge audience wasn't in the mood. As they used to say on *This Hour Has 22 Minutes*, "Not everyone may share this sense of humour."

The next morning I read a couple of newspapers over breakfast and scanned "National Newswatch" on the Internet but didn't see anything indicating I was about to cause a national sensation. I also ran through my email. There wasn't much, but I should have paid closer attention to a message from a Canadian graduate student at Michigan State University, excoriating my views on child pornography. She referred to a video from last night that she said was making the rounds on social media. Of course, she was referring to Arnell Tailfeathers's YouTube posting. If I'd been in campaign mode, I would have reacted; but in academic mode I didn't think much about it and didn't bother to look at the video on my iPad. Because of my appearances in the media, I frequently attract hostile email and social media postings, but they normally don't amount to anything of importance and I don't pay much attention to them.

With the benefit of hindsight, I wish I had gone back upstairs to my motel room and turned it into a war room. I could have used my iPad to find out what was percolating on the Internet. I could have answered email requests for interviews. I could have called my university office to pick up voicemail messages from reporters and tried to get back to them. If I had done all that, I might have blunted the media story that was about to break out. But in my relaxed frame of mind, this never occurred to me. I had a lunch appointment in Calgary with some co-authors and a publisher's representative, and I was eager to get back for that; so I got in my car and drove away.

I left about 9 a.m., listening to *V is for Vengeance* in my car and enjoying the solitude. About a third of the way to Calgary, my car phone rang with a call from Vitor Marciano and Paul Hinman, senior assistants to Danielle Smith, the leader of the Wildrose Party. I don't give out my car phone number widely, but they had contacted my wife at home and got it from her. They weren't calling to ask what had happened or what I had meant to say; they were just delivering bad news. There was a major media storm – I had already been condemned by the premier of Alberta and the Prime Minister's Office – and they were cutting me loose too. Marciano, a lifetime political operative, was obviously enjoying the tough guy role: "I've got good news and bad news," he said. "The good news is that you're going to have lots more spare time. The bad news is that your career is over" (or words to that effect; I can't recall exactly what he said). Hinman must have thought he was showing concern about my soul by quoting a garbled version of Matthew 18:6, which in the King James Version reads, "But whoso shall offend one of these little ones which believe in me, it were better for him that a millstone were hanged about his neck, and that he were drowned in the depth of the sea." They then emailed me a "courtesy" version of Danielle Smith's media release, for me to read on my iPad after pulling off the highway:

> There is no language strong enough to condemn Dr. Flanagan's comments. Child pornography is a despicable crime that seriously harms all those involved, including the viewer. The viewing of child pornography first requires the production

of child pornography, which causes untold suffering and abuse towards children. In no uncertain terms, Wildrose condemns the production, transmission and viewing of child pornography.

Three years ago, Wildrose MLA Heather Forsyth put forward a private members bill compelling the mandatory reporting of child pornography and we were very proud that the bill received unanimous support in the Alberta Legislature. We await its proclamation.

To be clear, Dr. Flanagan does not speak for me or the Wildrose caucus and he will have no role – formal or informal – with our organization going forward.

Maybe I should have parked at that point and turned the car into a war room. I could have used my iPad and car phone to contact reporters and try to get my side of the story out. But I think it was already too late. Now that I had been condemned by leading politicians, the storyline had shifted. It was no longer just "Flanagan makes shocking comments"; it was now "Everyone disowns Flanagan." It only took about an hour for the story to blow up beyond anyone's control.

Of all the blows I had to take in this affair, Danielle's hurt the most. It was not just the over-the-top wording ("There is no language strong enough to condemn. . . ."). It was even more the fact that Danielle herself had not bothered to call me. If she had called and said, "Tom, your comments have created a huge problem for us," I would have immediately resigned from my small advisory role with the party and we could have worked out a statement. I've ridden in this rodeo before; I wouldn't have tried to stay around knowing my presence was causing a problem. But now she was treating me like something she had stepped in and had to wipe off her shoe.

Her failure to call kept gnawing at me, so I sent her an email late in the evening on March 1. She replied briefly that she was broken-hearted about the whole thing and that we would talk in a few months after the furore had died down. I haven't heard from her yet.

I kept driving, still listening to *V is for Vengeance,* till I got back to my university office shortly before noon and started to catch up on what people were saying about me. Andrew McDougall, communications director in the Prime Minister's Office, had tweeted: "Tom Flanagan's comments on child pornography are repugnant, ignorant, and appalling." Being called "ignorant" by a PR flack was a new experience for me but about par for what Stephen Harper's PMO has become. Alberta premier Alison Redford had said to reporters, "It turned my stomach. I'm absolutely disgusted by it. I think that it's a perfect example of people that take ideological arguments too far, and I have nothing else to say on it." Then there was an email from the Manning Centre, saying that I had been disinvited from their annual networking conference scheduled for March 8–9 in Ottawa. A few weeks previously the centre had asked me to be one of their speakers, as I had been several times before, and I had rearranged my schedule to make it possible. Ironically, the featured speaker at the conference was American libertarian Ron Paul, whose views on child pornography are similar to mine and who was the only Republican to vote against some of the more extreme and repressive legislation passed by Congress.

The CBC fired me with a statement that was moderate by comparison with those coming from political organizations:

> In light of recent remarks made by Tom Flanagan at the University of Lethbridge, CBC News has taken the decision to end our association with him as a commentator on *Power and Politics*.
>
> While we support and encourage free speech across the country and a diverse range of voices, we believe Mr. Flanagan's comments to have crossed the line and impacted his credibility as a commentator for us.

There was a trope in this statement that I would see repeatedly in the next few days: "We support free speech but. . . ." People like to say this just before unleashing reprisals against someone who has made use of the right to speak freely.

To their credit, several people from the CBC, including *Power and Politics* host Evan Solomon, had tried to call me that morning but had been unable to reach me because I was in my car. I guess they felt they had to do something even without being able to consult me because I was supposed to be on *Power and Politics* that afternoon. As soon as I got to my office, I talked to Evan on the phone, then wrote up a statement that the CBC agreed to post on its website:

I absolutely condemn the sexual abuse of children, including the use of children to produce pornography. These are crimes and should be punished under the law. Last night, in an academic setting, I raised a theoretical question about how far criminalization should extend toward the consumption of pornography. My words were badly chosen, and in the resulting uproar I was not able to express my abhorrence of child pornography and the sexual abuse of children. I apologize unreservedly to all who were offended by my statement, and most especially to victims of sexual abuse and their families.

I still wonder whether this was the right thing to do. I was following standard damage control doctrine, which is to apologize as quickly and fully as possible and then shut up, not to prolong the story by giving partial explanations and apologies that soon have to be supplemented or replaced. On the other hand, what was I really sorry for? I had made a tactical error in trying to reason with an angry mob, but that was a mistake in judgment, not a moral failing. There would have been nothing wrong with my words in a normal academic setting, if they had been properly understood as a provocative first move in a long discussion. *Taste in pictures*, the phrase I used in Lethbridge, reprising the phrase I had used in Winnipeg, *just pictures*, was classroom shock wording meant to stimulate discussion. I had no idea that Arnell Tailfeathers was recording me and would post a snippet on YouTube under a misleading tagline. What exactly should be your responsibility when people are offended by words attributed to you ("okay with child pornography") but that you never said? Ken Westhues, a Canadian sociologist who has written extensively on mobbing in academia, emailed me that I shouldn't have apologized, that in a mobbing situation it only makes things worse. I suspect he's right.

By choosing to work on an apology for the CBC website, I missed my chance to have any voice in the statement that the University of Calgary was putting out. My department head, Brenda O'Neill, who has been very supportive throughout, came to my office and told me that the statement was being drafted right now and asked me if I wanted to be consulted, but I couldn't do two things at once. I mistakenly assumed that the university would put out its usual boilerplate – "Dr. Flanagan's views are his own and do not represent the University of Calgary." I never dreamed that President Elizabeth Cannon would put out a statement creating the impression across the country that I was being pushed into retirement because of what I had said in Lethbridge. I discuss this at length in the chapter on academic freedom.

Needless to say, my voicemail and email inbox were full of requests for interviews from reporters, but I didn't accept any after putting out my CBC statement. If I were superhuman, maybe I could have gone out, given my side of the story, and helped to produce a more balanced narrative in the media. But not only was it late in the game for that, I was shell-shocked and didn't know what to say. The whole episode was surreal to me. I was just an individual, with no staff to brief me about what was going on or devise media strategies. I decided it was better to say nothing, so I went over to the university's fitness centre for a workout, hoping that exercise would bring down the adrenalin level.

I spent the rest of the afternoon fending off more media invitations and making brief responses to the messages of support that were flooding in by email, telephone, or a simple knock at the door. It was amazingly different from what had happened in the Julian Assange episode. Then I had been overwhelmed with hostile, angry messages, even death threats. This time the emails and phone calls were 95 percent positive. Some expressed support for my doubts as to whether imprisonment should be the mandatory punishment for simple possession or viewing of child pornography. Others said they agreed with the law as is but expressed amazement that I was being mobbed for simply asking questions about legislation. My favourite was from a young political scientist teaching at an Ontario university, who wrote:

> I'm best described as a green social democrat. I'm also a lesbian in favour of an activist judiciary that strives to protect minority rights. This to say that we are probably not natural allies on most matters of public significance! . . . This must be a difficult time for you but please know that you have supporters. Even on the other side of the political spectrum.

Yet the flow of support, crucial as it was, was punctuated with more bad news that afternoon, as speaking invitations started to be cancelled. Universities were the first to cancel after political parties and the CBC had shown the way and after my own university had practically disowned me. I thought universities, of all institutions, would take the time to ask me what had happened, and not just act on media accounts of a YouTube video. Wrong again.

Media coverage on Thursday, February 28, took the form of radio and TV news, as well as website postings. On Friday, March 1, there began a veritable avalanche of print media all over the country that lasted all weekend, condemning me in front-page news stories as well as op-eds. I confess I didn't read most of it. I stayed off Internet news aggregator sites, and I think my wife must have intercepted the newspapers delivered to our home. The main themes were that my career was over (true in a restricted sense because I had already been planning to retire from teaching undergraduates); that my views on child pornography were out of date (whatever that meant); that child pornography was evil (with which I agreed); that I was wrong to say that child pornography should be legalized and that it was a victimless crime (I had never said either); and that I had long been a general pain in the ass (maybe true, depending on one's taste in infotainment).

This weekend was undoubtedly the lowest point in a career of many ups and downs, but encouraging signs were also present from the beginning, even beyond the email that was streaming in. As early as Thursday, Michael Taube posted an editorial on the *Ottawa Citizen* website in which he defended the criminalization of child pornography but also defended my right to raise questions about it. On Friday, Barbara Kay sent me a note of support and also posted a supportive column on the *National Post* website: "A distinguished career vanishes with the wind." I didn't much care for the title added by the editor because my career as a writer and commentator on public affairs is going to continue, even if I am reducing my teaching load; but the column itself was superb. Barbara agreed with me about the futility of imprisoning people merely for looking at child pornography, and she forcefully condemned the mobbing to which I was being subjected. Barbara's son Jonathan, the comment editor of the *National Post*, also had a column that day: "The mobbing of Tom Flanagan is unwarranted and cruel," in which he pointed out that my fragmentary remarks might mean many different things, and that one should give me a chance to explain before passing judgment. Even more importantly, he offered me space in the *National Post* to explain my position.

Now I had a chance to fight back, especially since Jaime Watt, Canada's leading practitioner of crisis communications, had privately offered to give me advice. I can't say I knew Jaime well, though we had crossed swords in two political campaigns. In 2004, my Team Harper had beaten his Team Belinda; and in 2012, he had paid me back by helping to rescue Alison Redford's foundering campaign in the last two weeks. In my eyes, his offer of help made him a modern reincarnation of the Good Samaritan.

After a systematic review of the media coverage, Jaime said it was the worst he had ever seen; so over the weekend, he and his colleague Carrie Kormos worked with me to develop a plan for fighting back. We settled on a strategy of doing three high-quality media hits to let me tell my own story in my own way. First, I would accept the offer from Jonathan Kay to write something for the *National Post*. That turned out to be a fourteen-hundred-word essay published Monday, March 4, in which I explained what had happened at Lethbridge and what my views on child pornography really are – that I think it's a great evil and appropriately subject to criminal penalties but that mandatory minimum prison terms may not be the best way of dealing with the lowest levels of offence, such as simple possession and viewing. There are, after all, many criminal sanctions in addition to prison, including probation, fines, community service, house arrest, mandatory therapy, and sentencing circles. In a humane society, prison should be the last resort, not the first, for people who have not directly harmed others.

The second media hit was a twenty-minute interview with Steve Paikin on *The Agenda*, which runs nightly on TVO. Though the audience is small, Paikin commands a lot of respect as a tough but fair interviewer. To get a larger audience, we might have preferred the CBC, with someone like Evan Solomon asking the questions, but the CBC refused to do it. Paikin did push me hard, but he also gave me plenty of leeway to answer his questions, so the interview served its purpose. It was aired Tuesday, March 5, my sixty-ninth birthday.

Third was a long feature interview for *Maclean's Magazine*, conducted by Anne Kingston. *Maclean's* is Canada's only weekly news magazine and one of the largest-circulation periodicals in the country. It was particularly useful to be able to tell my story there because printed magazines often sit around for weeks or months after delivery. People may read them in doctor's offices and beauty parlours, coffee shops and waiting rooms, so readership continues to build long after the date of publication.

After my quick trip to Toronto for the interviews with Steve Paikin and Anne Kingston, I did no more media, just hoping that what I had done would gradually influence opinion, and I believe there was a gradual effect. Many people have mentioned to me that they had a better idea of what it was all about after having read or seen one of these media hits. But of course, not everyone was swayed. Danielle Smith said that my media explanation "changes nothing for me. The comments that he made last week were completely unacceptable and appalling, and I don't think there's any way you can talk your way into having Albertans believe anything that was said was reasonable." For reasons I still don't understand, Danielle not only tried to bury me but also danced on the grave. Harper's PMO at least said nothing further after the first nasty tweet.

Fortunately, however, I was starting to get a lot of help from other authors – some friends, some people I had never met – expressing their own views in the media (a list of people who wrote on my behalf is included in the Acknowledgements at the end of the book). Only someone who has been through a mobbing experience can understood how important it is to have others show support.

Every public word of support, sympathy, and understanding was important, but I do want to say something more about three of these interventions because they were so unexpected and therefore so doubly welcome. Brenda Cossman is a University of Toronto law professor and lesbian activist who probably disagrees with almost everything I have ever done or said in public life. But she made a point of agreeing with me that "there is a lot to say about Canada's child pornography law." Conrad Black epitomizes recovery after suffering reverses that would have broken most men. And Michael Enright is a star performer for the CBC, which rushed to disown me on the morning of February 28. I can't resist quoting something Enright said about me on *Sunday Edition*: "Some of the things Flanagan puts forward run from the inane to the outrageous. Most are fascinating." Anyone who knows me would agree with the first sentence. Others will have to decide whether the second sentence is true.

Media condemnation was waning when Preston Manning gave it one more turn of the screw. In his concluding remarks at his conference on March 9, Manning held up my alleged views on child pornography as an object lesson of what conservative parties and organizations have to avoid: "Conservative governments, parties, and campaigns simply cannot afford to be blindsided and discredited by these incidents when the individuals involved are connected with those governments, with those parties, and with those campaigns. . . ." Manning also referred to his own past difficulties as Reform Party leader in dealing with candidates and other party members who made extreme statements.

Although Manning's statement gave me a couple more days of unfavourable publicity, there was another side to his conference, less covered in the media, that had considerable significance to me. Marco Navarro-Génie, director of research for the Frontier Centre for Public Policy and a former student of mine, quickly ordered a batch of lapel buttons with my face and name and passed them out at the networking conference. I'm told that dozens, maybe hundreds of people wore them. It was a sign that I still had friends, even if I had been denounced by the heads of organizations. Anyway, this was the last stage of the virtual mobbing. After the news coverage of the Manning Centre conference, a couple more columns appeared, but the public had obviously moved on to other bright shiny objects. I could be left in relative peace to think about the important questions discussed in the rest of this book.

## CHAPTER 3

# THE PANIC OVER PORNOGRAPHY

## You Got Trouble

*THE MUSIC MAN* IS A BELOVED STANDARD OF American musical comedy. "Professor" Harold Hill, a con man posing as a music instructor, comes to River City, Iowa, intending to persuade parents to pay for uniforms and instruments for a new boys' band and then skip town with the money. In one of the funniest scenes, he tells parents that a boys' band is just what they need to keep their sons away from the moral degradation of pool halls. In the language of contemporary social science, he creates a moral panic over the game of pool.

British sociologist Stanley Cohen brought the term *moral panic* into social science with his 1972 book *Folk Devils and Moral Panics: The Creation of the Mods and Rockers*. Mods and Rockers were two youth subcultures of 1960s Britain. Mods dressed in tweeds, listened to blues and jazz, and rode motor scooters; Rockers dressed in leather, listened to Elvis, and rode motorcycles. Fights between members of the groups were frequent at seaside resorts in 1964, leading to sensational headlines in the newspapers about the threat of youth violence to society. In revisiting his earlier work, Cohen has isolated five features that characterize moral panics:

1. Concern about a perceived threat to the social and moral order.

2. Outrage expressed at the "folk devils" (the demonic opposite of "folk heroes") who threaten the social order, such as teenaged gangs, drug dealers, and sexual predators. Outrage leads to suspension of normal standards of judgment, rationality, and due process in dealing with such folk devils.

3. Widespread agreement among elite groups who dominate the media that the threat is real and "something should be done."

4. Extreme exaggeration of the numbers of incidents and victims and the threat posed to social order.

5. Volatile eruption and disappearance of such episodes. The Mods and Rockers burst on the scene in the early 1960s, but a few years later no one knew who they were, except for those who had read Cohen's doctoral dissertation published in book form.

Scholars have applied the concept of moral panic to many notorious episodes. Most prominent in American history would be the Salem witch trials of 1692–93, which led to the execution of twenty-four "witches," mostly women. The accusations started with young girls accusing women of causing physical afflictions, and spread from there as the accused often confessed and named others, perhaps to avoid torture by the peine forte et dure (pressing by boards loaded with stones) that killed one accused. Much of the so-called evidence was "spectral evidence," that is, sights allegedly seen in visions. Fortunately, the hysteria waned after a year, when the authorities began to fear it could get completely out of control, and no one since then has been executed in the United States for the crime of witchcraft. The Salem witch trials perfectly illustrate everything established by Stanley Cohen as characteristic of moral panics.

Arthur Miller's play *The Crucible* (1953) dramatized the Salem trials but was also an allegory about the persecution of communists in contemporary America, led over several years by the House Un-American Activities Committee as well by the alcoholic Republican Senator from Wisconsin, "Tail Gunner Joe" McCarthy. Unlike Salem, where there was no actual problem of witchcraft, there had been a genuine problem of communist espionage in the United States. Alger Hiss really was a Soviet agent, and the Rosenbergs did actually give away atomic secrets. But the scale of such subversion was far smaller than implied by McCarthy's famous claim, never substantiated, to have a list of more than two hundred Soviet agents in his pocket. In spite of very limited evidence, the hunt for Soviet agents extended far beyond government offices. Many scientists, artists, writers, movie directors, professors, teachers, and other purveyors of ideas were hounded out of their careers, and even out of the country. Ironically, in the hunt for un-American subversives, truly un-American practices such as loyalty oaths and anonymous informants became common for a while in many professions. Today, Americans almost universally look back on this period with embarrassment and even horror, but the hysteria was unstoppable while it lasted.

A Canadian example would include the criminalization of opiates, cocaine, and marijuana. These substances were all legal in nineteenth-century Canada, as in most other countries. Cocaine was used in soft drinks, hence the name Coca-Cola. Laudanum – a potent concoction of alcohol and opium – was a common home remedy. Opium was first forbidden in Canada in 1908, following anti-Chinese riots. It was part of the general reaction against "unfair competition" from Chinese immigrants, who did indeed smoke opium. Cannabis was added to the list of illegal drugs in 1923, shortly after the publication of Emily Murphy's book *The Black Candle*, which had first appeared as a series of articles in *Maclean's Magazine* under the byline of "Janey Canuck." Murphy, the first female police magistrate in the British empire, stigmatized marijuana as a dangerous drug associated with undesirable Asian and black immigrants. In a broader sense, the banning of cannabis was part of the social hygiene agenda of progressive feminism, which also included prohibition of alcohol and eugenic sterilization of those deemed unfit to reproduce, along with many other reforms that today might still seem genuinely progressive.

The mood of hysteria that characterizes moral panics may exhaust itself quickly, as happened in Salem in 1693, but the effects can linger on for decades if politicians legislate in a spirit of moral panic. The eugenics legislation passed in Alberta in 1928 was not repealed until 1971. The use of cannabis is still a crime in Canada ninety years after the first legislation, and indeed the government has recently imposed a mandatory minimum prison sentence of six months for possession of six marijuana plants, considering that to be *prima facie* evidence of intention to traffic in the drug. So the concept of volatility has to be properly understood when applied to moral panics that result in legislation. The period of exaggerated emotion may be short, but it may result in a very long-lasting social consensus with a concomitant impact upon public policy.

Historian Philip Jenkins, in his book *Moral Panic: Changing Concepts of the Child Molester in Modern America,* has shown how all of this applies to the question of child pornography. Until about thirty years ago, there was no legal category of child pornography and little specialized discussion of it. There had long been legislation against pornography as well as against the sexual abuse of children, but the two were only recently fused to produce a joint category of concern.

A little historical perspective is necessary here. From the beginning of the twentieth century up to the late 1950s, adults who sought sexual relations with children were heavily stigmatized, often under quasi-medical terms such as *pervert* or *degenerate*. Pornography was also subject to legal barriers, including Criminal Code provisions, customs inspections, and rules regarding performances and exhibitions. Hollywood, under pressure from external bodies such as the Legion of

Decency, also had its own internal censorship mechanisms. Then came the Sixties, which really started in the late 1950s and carried on into the early 1970s. Suddenly, almost all sexual mores were relaxed. Divorce was made easier; contraception, abortion, and homosexuality were legalized; adultery, fornication, promiscuity, and free love were presented sympathetically, even glorified, in the mass media; obscenity laws ceased to be enforceable even when not repealed. Along with these changes, attitudes toward the sexual use of children seemed to soften. Harsh words such as *pervert* and *psychopath* gave way in the popular lexicon to softer terms such as *child molester* or *exhibitionist*. Books, magazines, and movies depicting childhood sexuality started to become readily available in North America, mostly imported from Europe. Culminating this trend was the 1987 foundation of the North American Man/Boy Love Association (NAMBLA), whose purpose was to lobby governments to lower the age of consent for sexual relations.

The counterattack, however, was already well under way. Feminism, which had seemed sexually libertarian in the Sixties, showed another side, redefining sexual intercourse as an act of power by men over women. "Women have very little idea of how much men hate them," wrote Germaine Greer in *The Female Eunuch*. Susan Brownmiller wrote that rape is "nothing more or less than a conscious process of intimidation by which all men keep all women in a state of fear." Robin Morgan said, "Pornography is the theory, rape is the practice."

The attitude that women were under siege and always at risk of violent attack had an important influence on the law. In

Canada, the concept of rape was taken out of the Criminal Code to be replaced by several levels of sexual assault. The point was to emphasize the feminist theory that rape is based on power and violence, not sexual desire. New offences of sexual harassment in the workplace and other public venues were inserted into all the human rights codes in Canada. In 1992, the Supreme Court's *Butler* decision upheld the Criminal Code prohibition of obscenity on the novel feminist argument that pornography is bad not because it corrupts morals but because it is degrading to women. Non-legislative initiatives were important too, such as shelters for abused women and take-back-the-night marches. In this climate of feminist fear-mongering against allegedly powerful men, protection of children from sexual abuse took on new meaning as an extension of protecting women from the malignant patriarchy.

The ideological atmosphere provided the ambiance for a moral panic over daycare centres. "Children always tell the truth became the motto of the movement," just as "women never lie about accusations of rape" was the feminist mantra. The best-known American case involved the McMartin daycare centre in San Diego. A mother later determined to be mentally disturbed claimed in 1983 that her son had been molested at the daycare. Police brought in special investigators from a sexual abuse clinic to interview hundreds of children and parents. Their suggestive interrogation methods elicited fantastic stories, for which there was no physical evidence, involving torture, mutilation, and telekinesis. Nonetheless, members of the McMartin family and their employees were put through a trial lasting several years. In 1990, all were acquitted or had their charges dropped, although one family member spent five years in jail without ever being convicted of anything.

Hundreds of copycat cases swept the United States and spilled into other countries. The most famous case in Canada occurred at a daycare centre in Martensville, Saskatchewan, where a mother charged that children were being sexually abused in fantastic ways by the "Brotherhood of the Ram" at a "Devil Church." The son of the owner was indicted and convicted. Several other people, including five police officers, were also charged, but the prosecutions were dropped after the RCMP made a more thorough investigation and concluded that local police and prosecuting attorneys had been led astray by disturbed adults and imaginative children. The provincial government and local authorities eventually paid compensation to the victims of malicious prosecution, though it took years of legal wrangling to achieve that result.

Looking back on these cases now, one is tempted to ask, "How could they have happened?" How could literally impossible charges involving satanic cults, extraterrestrial beings, murders without corpses, and torture without scars ever have been taken seriously by lawyers, psychiatrists, social workers, and police? This was, after all, twentieth-century North America, not tenth-century Europe. Yet people went to jail, families and businesses were bankrupted, careers were destroyed. It is tragic testimony to what otherwise rational people will do in the midst of moral panic.

An important feature of the daycare abuse panic was the coalescence of feminists, moral conservatives, and law enforcement agencies. Feminists were pursuing their anti-patriarchal agenda, which moral and religious conservatives would not have approved if they had understood it. Yet conservatives had been traumatized by the sexual libertarianism of the Sixties and saw a chance to strike back through the protection of children. They might not be able to reverse abortion and divorce on demand, but they could stand up to defend the family. Charges of satanic rituals in the abuse of children may have even seemed plausible to some fundamentalist Christians, just as charges against Jews for kidnapping and torturing Christian children seemed plausible in the Middle Ages. For their part, law enforcement agencies make their living enforcing the law. Allegations of satanic sexual abuse at daycare centres opened up a new market for them – new investigative officers, new task forces, special training in esoteric methods of interrogation.

The panic over child pornography coincided with many other concerns about sexual offences against children – sexual abuse in orphanages and residential schools; pedophile priests in Catholic parishes; child-molesting Boy Scout leaders and hockey coaches; and, every parent's worst nightmare, occasional cases of kidnapped children who were raped and murdered. Children seemed to be under threat of sexual abuse at every turn.

Jenkins suggests that all this concern, and the daycare sex abuse panic in particular, was underpinned by demographic and workplace changes. By the 1980s, the huge baby boom cohort no longer consisted of teenagers looking for sexual novelty but parents worrying about how to raise children in the sexually libertarian world the boomers had created. Also, mothers with young children were increasingly entering the workforce, causing children to spend more time with adults other than their own parents. At all times there are moral entrepreneurs talking about sexual threats to children, but the demographic trends of the 1980s created a larger audience for their message of ubiquitous danger. And protection against sexual abuse also serves as a kind of discipline for children themselves, making it harder for them to engage in sexual experiments as they enter their teenaged years.

If Jenkins is correct in his analysis, then fears about childhood sexuality and demands for institutionalized protective measures will persist because women's entry into the workforce seems to be permanent. Indeed, that prediction seems to have been borne out. The daycare panic finally collapsed because of the extremism, even craziness, of many of its allegations; but draconian legislation against child sexual abuse remains on the books while penalties and investigative measures are periodically ratcheted upward. Harsh laws against child pornography are part of a legal matrix including stiffer penalties for all sexual offences, sexual offender registries, and security checks for those who want to work with children.

More or less contemporaneous with the daycare panic was a related moral panic over "recovered memory syndrome." The key text in this movement was the 1988 best-seller *The Courage to Heal* by lesbian activists Ellen Bass and Laura Davis. Neither woman had any training in psychology, psychotherapy, or other sciences dealing with the brain or the mind. Nonetheless, they popularized the vaguely Freudian thesis that memories of sexual abuse were so traumatic that they could be completely repressed for years or decades, then surface again, particularly if therapists used the right techniques.

Inspired by *The Courage to Heal* and similar texts, thousands of young people, particularly those treated by psychotherapists specializing in the new methodology, started to accuse fathers, grandfathers, uncles, and older brothers of unspeakable acts of childhood sexual abuse. Some of the charges involved satanic rituals and tortures as lurid as anything in the daycare repertoire of charges. Allegations were mostly against men, but mothers, grandmothers, aunts, and older sisters inevitably got drawn in because they had not stopped the crimes or allegedly had even joined in. As with the daycare fiasco, the panic over recovered memory syndrome eventually burnt itself out, thanks in no small part to the efforts of courageous scientists such as the University of Washington's Elizabeth Loftus, who in her 1994 book, *The Myth of Repressed Memory,* debunked the unproved theories behind the movement. Yet enormous damage was done as thousands of families were torn apart by allegations of long-forgotten sexual abuse. Some unfortunate people, the real victims of the panic, were sent to jail over charges that would never have been proven under traditional standards of testimony and evidence, just as in the daycare panic.

Both the daycare panic and the recovered memory panic were about allegations of deeds, not words and pictures, but child pornography was also involved in the tableau. Complainants often alleged that their sexual abuse had been photographed or recorded in some way. There were also many allegations that victims had been passed around within pedophile "rings," that photographs and videos had been used to lure them in, to groom them on how to play their part, and to advertise their availability to other members of these rings. In spite of sensational headlines in the media, repeated investigations by law enforcement agencies have never uncovered anything resembling a true organized pedophile ring. One set of allegations in Cornwall, Ontario, persisted for twenty years, culminating in a judicial inquiry costing $53 million, but no "ring" was ever discovered.

Of course, the sexual abuse of children sometimes happens and is on rare occasions accompanied by torture and murder. However, all the talk of satanic rituals, recovered memories, and pedophile rings was as nonsensical as the spectral evidence submitted in the Salem witch trials, and the craziness eventually led these moral panics to collapse. Yet they left a legacy of fear and concern over juvenile sexuality in which the child pornographer, powerfully assisted by the Internet, could become a new folk devil.

## Child Pornography Legislation

Historically there was no special legislation for child pornography; it was simply included under the category of obscenity, which was covered in the Criminal Code of

Canada, as in most other countries. Special legislation on child pornography was a reaction to the moral panics of the 1980s. Each country has its own story and timetable of how legislators responded to these moral panics; here I will trace what happened in Canada.

The Canadian story began in early 1981, when the recently re-elected Liberal government of Pierre Trudeau appointed a blue-ribbon Committee on Sexual Offences against Children and Youths, chaired by University of Toronto professor of medicine Robin Badgley. It is usually known simply as the Badgley Committee. Its 1984 report was a model of thoroughness, totalling 1,314 pages. About 200 pages were devoted to pornography and obscenity in general, including one chapter on child pornography.

The Badgley Committee's research findings on child pornography were quite restrained. It reported that there was no Canadian industry producing and distributing child pornography for commercial profit, nor was child pornography a major part of the lucrative adult pornography business. Books, magazines, and videos containing child pornography were sometimes imported from the United States and Europe, either through the mail or shipments of goods. Canadian authorities could not hope to stamp out the flow completely, but they certainly had tools to limit it. Beyond that, sex offenders sometimes made their own pornographic materials, which were occasionally used in the seduction of youth, but the committee did not find evidence that large numbers of children were put at risk in this way. The technical part of the report gives the impression that child pornography in Canada was an evil that required counter-measures, but not that it was a widespread threat to children (all this, of course, was before personal computers and the Internet came into use).

The committee's policy recommendations, however, went far beyond its moderate research findings. They are worth quoting at length because they have set the parameters of public debate up to the present:

> In the Committee's judgment, the need for explicit and severe legal sanctions against persons involved in the making, distribution, sale, or importation of child pornography is compelling for several reasons.
>
> First, child pornography is produced directly through the sexual abuse of young persons. . . .
>
> Second, child pornography constitutes a permanent record of a child's sexual exploitation and the harm and humiliation to the child are exacerbated by the circulation, distribution, or sale of such materials.
>
> Third, materials which depict children engaged in sexual conduct are often solicited by adults who use the materials to persuade other children to engage in similar conduct or who are themselves child molesters. The Committee's findings in this regard bear out this fact. The Committee's findings showed that this does happen, but not how often. In particular, these findings buttress the argument for enacting express legal sanctions against the importation and possession of child pornography.

Fourth, the distribution network for child pornography must be shut down if the production of such materials, which itself requires the sexual exploitation of children, is to be effectively controlled. Legal sanctions directed at each link of the chain of distribution would help. . . .

Fifth, the importation, circulation, distribution or sale of child pornography provides economic and other motives for the continued production of such materials and, in effect, guarantees additional child sexual abuse to that end. In the Committee's judgment, the only effective way to curtail the production of child pornography, and to eradicate it from the Canadian market entirely, is to attach criminal consequences to the conduct of each participant in the process, from the importer or maker of child pornography to the ultimate consumer of child pornography, and to all intermediate parties who are culpable.

Sixth, the existing *Criminal Code* framework relating to obscene publications is inadequate to deal with the special circumstances attending the making and distribution of child pornography. . . . In reference to child pornography, it is the circumstances of its production, namely, the sexual exploitation of young persons, which is a fundamental basis of proscription.

These influential recommendations went far beyond the committee's research findings and contain some obvious fallacies. First, it is sometimes but not always true that "child pornography is produced directly through the sexual abuse of young persons." Some child pornography takes the form of written stories, paintings and drawings, cartoons, comics, and photographs of adults posing as teenagers. And if it is not true that children have always been abused in the making of child pornography, one of the main reasons behind the committee's recommendation to punish simple possession loses its force. Moreover, though the committee's researchers had found that commercial production and distribution of child pornography hardly existed in Canada, the committee recommended prosecution of voyeurs as a way to eradicate the (non-existent) market.

The committee's final point is highly important, yet its importance is not at all obvious to someone who is not a lawyer or who has not read the legal literature. If child pornography is a type of obscenity, it has some protection under Canadian law and the Charter of Rights and Freedoms. The courts have held that Parliament can legislate about obscenity, but that not all sexual depictions are obscene. Many factors come into the evaluation, including content, context, and audience. Child pornography legislation, in contrast, is far more absolutist. All depictions of anyone under eighteen that can be construed as sexual now belong to the category of child pornography and can be punished as such. This approach is far more aggressive than that found in the older law of obscenity. It flows from removing child pornography from the category of obscenity, which was long regulated by the Criminal Code and which therefore had accumulated an interpretive and qualifying body of jurisprudence.

Consistent with its analysis, the committee proposed draft legislation that was a radical break with the past. Any visual representation of "explicit sexual conduct" by any person under eighteen would be forbidden under the Criminal Code. Penalties including imprisonment up to ten years would extend to making, distributing, selling, exhibiting, and possessing such material. Although radical by past standards, this was considerably less than what the law has subsequently become in Canada. It covered only "visual representations," so did not include novels and stories. It did not impose mandatory minimum jail sentences, leaving judges free to impose other penalties such as fines and conditional sentences. And it treated mere possession, without intention to distribute, exhibit, or sell, more leniently. Simple possession would still be criminalized, but it would be a lesser offence punishable on summary conviction, which meant a simpler process and lower penalties.

The committee frankly admitted that it had faced internal disagreements over how to treat mere possession:

> The Committee had no difficulty in agreeing that legal sanctions at each link from production through importation, distribution and sale were required to increase the protection to children exploited in the preparation and depictions of pornographic activities. There was sharp disagreement, however, over whether this should extend to simple possession of such material.
>
> Those Members who favoured this argued it was the logical extension of the chain of legal sanctions. Those

members who opposed it reflected a major concern about intrusion into the privacy of the home, regressive moves towards more control of personal choice and life-style and an extension of censorship principles. The Committee's review of these issues reflects the divided opinions held by various groups in Canadian society.

Making simple possession a lesser but still criminal offence seems to have been, at least in part, a compromise between the different points of view represented on the committee.

The report of the Badgley Committee, which had been appointed by a Liberal government, arrived in Ottawa just as the Conservative government of Brian Mulroney was about to come to power. The Conservatives took their full nine years in office to craft a legislative response. Child pornography bills introduced in 1986 and 1987 generated a lot of controversy among arts, media, and civil liberties groups worried about censorship, and they never were brought to a final vote. Then the government became preoccupied with a heavy political agenda, including Meech Lake and the Charlottetown Accords, free trade with the United States, the goods and services tax (GST), and abortion. Mulroney finally grasped the nettle in May 1993, when public opinion was distracted by the Conservative leadership race between Jean Charest and Kim Campbell. Bringing in child pornography legislation seems to have been more a matter of housekeeping than a major issue in Mulroney's mind; he didn't even mention it in his thousand-page memoirs.

On May 13, Justice Minister Pierre Blais introduced Bill C-128, An Act to amend the Criminal Code and the Customs Tariff (child pornography and corrupting morals). After perfunctory debate in the House of Commons, it was supported by all five parties – one of the rare times that the Progressive Conservatives, Liberals, NDP, Bloc Québécois, and Reform agreed on anything. After equally quick scrutiny in the Senate, it received royal assent on June 23, showing how quickly the political process can move when politicians want to take something off the table.

Bill C-128 made certain changes to the Badgley recommendations. It included not only "visual representations" but also written material "that advocates or counsels sexual activity with a person under the age of eighteen years that would be an offence under this Act." And it offered the option of summary conviction for distributing child pornography as well as merely possessing it. But the broad outlines were the same – criminalize child pornography, including simple possession, and provide for stiff, but not mandatory, jail terms. There was a fair amount of criticism from arts and media groups, including the CBC, that the bill was too inclusive and was being rushed through Parliament just to provide talking points in the looming federal elections. General public opinion, however, seemed supportive, as shown by the unanimous vote of all parties at third reading in the House of Commons.

The new legislation was quickly tested in court. In 1995, British Columbia resident John Robin Sharpe was charged with both simple possession and intent to distribute child pornography. Representing himself, Sharpe argued that the legislation violated the guarantee of "freedom of thought, belief, opinion, and expression" in section 2(b) of the Charter of Rights and Freedoms. The British Columbia Court of Appeal agreed with Sharpe as far as simple possession was concerned. Justice Anne Rowles wrote in her concurring opinion:

> The detrimental effects of s. 163.1(4) on freedom of expression and personal privacy are substantial. By providing a sentence of incarceration for the possession of recorded thoughts and expression, including one's own thoughts and expression, the legislation trenches deeply upon the core values enshrined in the Charter and essential to a free and democratic society. The definition of child pornography in s. 163.1(1) captures a vast range of materials, a significant portion of which cannot be shown to pose a danger to children, especially when the materials remain in the private possession of their creator. The far-reaching definition of child pornography, in the context of a simple possession offence, also raises the spectre that legitimate and non-harmful expression will be chilled as individuals are forced, in the words of the trial judge, to become their own censors.

In 2001, however, the Supreme Court of Canada reversed the B.C. Court of Appeal and upheld the Mulroney government's legislation while carving out an exception for materials created by a defendant solely for personal use, for example, a diary.

In addition to the *Sharpe* case, which had a very high profile in public opinion, there were many instances in which the courts imposed conditional sentences without jail time but involving restrictions on computer use and requirements to stay away from areas frequented by children. Judges were applying the law as worded but seemed reluctant to impose the most severe penalties. This created a political opportunity for the Canadian Alliance, and later the Conservative Party of Canada, to demand that the law be made more stringent so that judges could not evade it.

In the early days of the Reform Party, criminal justice issues barely registered on the dial, but Preston Manning and his caucus became more interested after the Charlottetown Accord was defeated and constitutional questions seemed to recede in importance. Reform turned itself into the Canadian Alliance, and Stockwell Day became leader in 2000, giving new leverage to the social conservatives, for whom child pornography was an iconic issue. It was not without risk, of course; I have already mentioned how Day undermined his own leadership by accusing Red Deer lawyer Lorne Goddard of supporting child pornography because he was defending a client accused of possession. Yet the issue was popular with many voters, and the Alliance/Conservatives kept badgering the Liberals to toughen up the law. After several iterations, Paul Martin's government got Bill C-2 through Parliament in 2005, which first introduced mandatory minimum jail terms for simple possession – forty-five days for an indictable offence and fourteen days for summary conviction. There was not a recorded vote at third reading because no party chose to oppose the bill in its final form. The Conservatives were

pushing the hardest, and no one else wanted to appear supportive of child pornography.

Not content with that victory, the Conservative majority
government made the law even more draconian in 2012 by
means of the omnibus Bill C-10, which raised the mandatory
minimum term of imprisonment for simple possession to six
months. This time the opposition parties voted against the
bill, although not especially over the issue of prison terms for
viewers of child pornography. As an omnibus bill, C-10 also
contained a number of other punitive measures, most notably
a mandatory minimum sentence for possession of six or more
marijuana plants.

I now blush to admit that, as Stephen Harper's chief of
staff and campaign manager during the years 2001–2005, I was
marginally involved in this populist rush toward ever more
draconian legislation. Since I was dealing with organization
and fundraising rather than policy, I was only barely aware of
our position on child pornography, but I had no objection to it
at the time. Though I hardly thought much about it, I'm sure I
saw it then not only as good politics but as a justified punishment for despicable criminals – the usual conservative and
Conservative attitude toward crime of all sorts.

I honestly can't say when or why I started to have second
thoughts. The rhetorical question I posed at the University
of Manitoba in November 2009 just popped out spontaneously; it wasn't based on any research I had been doing, or
even on any conscious thought. I wasn't deeply informed
about the merits of the debate or the history of the issue in

Canada. I don't think I gave the matter any further conscious thought until that night in Lethbridge in February 2013 when I was asked to explain what I had said in Manitoba. But the Incident has forced me to read and think much more about child pornography. As I will explain at greater length in the next chapter, I think Canada has gone too far in several respects while pursuing the laudable goal of repressing child pornography. Mandatory minimum prison time for simple possession is only one of several ways in which our law may have overreached.

Canadians are usually a moderate people. As Preston Manning often jokes, "Why did the Canadian cross the road? To get to the middle." Canadian legislation is usually full of qualifications and caveats that take account of real-world complexity. But moral panic can cause even the most judicious people to resort to extreme solutions. And that, I think, is what has happened here. The moral panics of the 1980s over claims of recovered memories, sexual abuse in daycare centres, and pedophile rings formed the matrix from which child pornography legislation emerged. Producers, dealers, and even viewers of child pornography became folk devils, to be punished no matter what the cost in money or damage to our legal traditions. The mood of hysteria subsided, as it always does, but it left a framework for political opportunism to connect the dots and fill in the blanks.

## CHAPTER 4

# THE MECHANICS OF MOBBING

## Triggering Moral Aggression

MORAL PANICS ARE ONE OF THE SOURCES OF mobbing. One who questions dogmas established in the wake of moral panic can seem like a threat to the social order, a threat to be repelled by collective action.

The notion of mobbing is not new, but it did not become a subject of scientific and academic study until the twentieth century. Nobel Prize–winning ethologist Konrad Lorenz drew attention to it, particularly in birds such as crows and geese (even writing in German, Lorenz chose to use the English word *mob*). Crows, for example, will sometimes gang up to harass hawks, owls, cats, and other predators. Crows will also stage collective attacks on a member of the flock that has fallen into disfavour for some reason, driving away or even killing the unfortunate bird. The study of mobbing in various mammal and avian species is now a recognized part of the science of ethology, or animal behaviour.

Closer to the human species, our chimpanzee cousins have been known to mob predators such as leopards. Male chimpanzees form coalitions in their struggle for dominance, which is not the same thing as mobbing, but both males and females will sometimes gang up to punish a male who has become too much of a bully.

Human beings engage in mobbing, as in the example of lynching, which tends to occur whenever formal mechanisms of law enforcement are weak or protection is not extended to unpopular minorities. Mobbing is part of a suite of human behaviours that evolutionary psychologists call moral aggression; other examples of moral aggression include gossip, bullying, criminal justice, and warfare. Gossip often involves passing on scandalous news about people who flout moral norms and conventions, thus punishing them by damaging their reputation. Bullies often see themselves not so much as picking on the weak as imposing retribution on those who don't measure up to usual standards. Criminal justice is a formalized system of using the state to inflict punishment that would otherwise come from vigilantes and lynch mobs. In the minds of cunning statesmen, war might be undertaken for all sorts of practical reasons, but getting support for it at the popular level always requires perception of wrongs that need to be righted.

According to evolutionary psychologists, the capacity for moralistic aggression has become entrenched in the human genome because it can foster the rule-following behaviour that is so necessary in our social species. What form it will take depends on surrounding social circumstances. As Harvard psychologist Steven Pinker has shown in his 2011 book *The Better Angels of Our Nature,* the combination of strong centralized government and a general softening of social mores has led to a decline of violence in modern times. Thus mobbing in the physical sense of lynching is much less common than it used to be. But at the same time new opportunities for mobbing have opened up. Social media, combining on the Internet with older mass media, provide an almost cost-free venue for expressing moral outrage. Voilà virtual mobbing! Press a few keys and you can join in denouncing someone you've never met but who is reported to have said something offensive.

In the age of the Internet, virtual mobbing is the inevitable doppelgänger of moral panic. Whether verified or not, stories of outrage rocket around the world at 300 million metres per second. People make sense of them by fitting them into pre-existing frameworks of evil and threat. There's no time for research or reflection when the social order is threatened on all sides by folk devils – child pornographers, drug dealers, and jihadis in the imagination of the right; racists, big corporations, and the tar sands in the imagination of the left. Even if the law no longer allows us to stone those folk devils, we can metaphorically do the equivalent by online denunciation.

Since the 1950s, a large social-science literature on mobbing in the workplace as well as other human collectives, such as residential schools and military units, has developed. Victims of workplace mobbing, including mobbing in universities, often have three characteristics in common. First, they belong to a racial, linguistic, or religious minority. Second, their achievements are higher than average. Third, they have challenged conventional wisdom or morality in some way – espousing an unpopular opinion, ignoring workplace norms or union rules, working too hard in class (the fabled "curve buster").

It is not hard to see how these characteristics work in tandem to unleash group hostility. A member of a minority is likely to seem different and, as a practical matter, to have fewer defenders. High achievement can make one a target of envy and resentment. And challenging conventional wisdom or behavioural rules will obviously evoke some opposition.

Now, what happened to me in the Incident was not workplace mobbing in the usual sense. I had no problems, at least none that I'm aware of, with fellow faculty members at the University of Calgary. I suffered a kind of virtual mobbing, in which I was attacked suddenly and from all sides in the media. That did lead to a bit of unpleasantness with my employer, described in more detail in the chapter on academic freedom, but the main damage was to my reputation as expressed in the media. When crows mob a member of the flock, they dive-bomb and strike with beak and claws. In contrast, human beings can now mob without any physical presence at all, indeed without having any personal knowledge of the target.

It is striking that, even if virtual mobbing is different from normal workplace mobbing, the same victim characteristics seem to be at work. I am not a member of a visible minority, but I am an American immigrant to Canada; and Americans are

one of the few groups in Canada against which expression of
hostility is still tolerated. I am still sometimes identified in the
media as "the American political scientist Tom Flanagan," even
though I have been a Canadian citizen since 1974. I have
appeared prominently in many public forums, including newspapers, television, courtrooms, and political campaigns. As a
political conservative, I am almost always at odds with the conventional wisdom of the Canadian academy and media; and as a
natural contrarian, I am sometimes at odds with fellow conservatives, leaving me dangerously exposed to mobbing.

## The Logic of Human Sacrifice

The virtual mobbing that I underwent was not just a random
collection of individual attacks. It was a highly structured,
layered onslaught of several different types of attacks and
attackers. To understand what happened, we have to drill
down through the layers of social media, mainstream media,
politicians, governmental organizations, and people at large.

At the core was the action of the two Idle No More activists who posted the YouTube clip taglined "Tom Flanagan
okay with child pornography." They claimed at one point to
be aspiring journalists and not to have intended to trap me.
Maybe that was even the subjective reality in their minds. But
they were not following any reputable journalistic norms
when they concocted a question unrelated to the subject of
my talk, recorded me without asking my consent or even

informing me, failed to carry out a follow-up interview, and posted their recorded snippet over a completely misleading tagline. This was an attack pure and simple, as they in fact later admitted to the Aboriginal newspaper *Alberta Sweetgrass*. Indeed, Arnell Tailfeathers illustrated that during the event when he recorded himself saying, "Gotcha, Tom."

But defamatory trash gets posted on social media every day. What turned this into a major story was that the mainstream media picked it up and ran with it without source-checking. They immediately went to the political parties and organizations with which I had been associated in the past, asking for comment, without asking me what I had meant to say. Some did try to reach me, but I was in my car for two and half hours, and apparently no one could wait that long to post their stories. By the time any reporter could reach me, the story was not what I had said but how others had reacted to it. At that point, explaining what I been trying to say would only have heaped more fuel on the fire; the damage had been done.

I doubt the media were motivated by personal hostility to me. I am well known within the media because over the years I have spent thousands of hours answering their questions, mostly for free. Some of my conservative friends say I was ambushed by the liberal media, but I don't think that's right. I think the correct explanation lies in the competitive pressure of our accelerated news cycle, combined with the lure of a "gotcha" story, which the media love because it is so easy to report.

But the media by themselves couldn't have engineered this story. What gave it legs was the series of over-the-top denunciations by all the political leaders for whom I had ever worked. In one sense, this was routine posturing by politicians against the backdrop of moral panic. Having created a moral panic over child pornography, politicians cannot afford to be caught offside. They feel they can't take time for critical analysis; they have to issue an immediate moral condemnation. The goal is not to understand what someone has tried to say but to lead the chorus of right-thinking people in denouncing evil. This background helps to explain the extraordinarily strong language that my former employers used to denounce me. I was painted as tolerant of child pornography, maybe even a personal consumer. I was now a "folk devil," and only the strongest language is appropriate for denouncing the devil. But beyond the overarching situation of moral panic and ritual denunciation, each political leader had specific reasons for weighing in.

For Alison Redford, the Progressive Conservative premier of Alberta, it was unbridled partisanship against the Official Opposition, the Wildrose Party. Relations between the two parties are unusually bad, even by today's degraded standards of civility; so Progressive Conservative leader Alison Redford will go to great lengths to damage Wildrose leader Danielle Smith and vice versa (so much for the utopian feminist dream that the presence of women will make politics less combative). Since it was well known that I had managed the recent campaign that had almost unseated Redford and the PCs, going after me was a way of going after Smith. There was no personal enmity between Redford and me. I was once in the same large room with her, but I had never spoken personally with her and had said very little about her in the media. To the extent that her attack on me was anything more than a moral panic reflex, it was pure political opportunism, a way of hurting her opponents.

Danielle Smith's motivation was different, though equally opportunistic. There wasn't any tension between us; in fact, I had recently spent a whole day with her, starting to map out the next Wildrose campaign for the 2016 provincial election. The source of her attack on me lies rather in certain things that happened in the final week of the 2012 campaign, when the Wildrose lead slipped away due to candidate gaffes. The main one was a year-old blog posting by Edmonton South candidate Allan Hunsperger, a Pentecostal minister. It was based on a sermon he had given at his church in Tofield, a small town outside of Edmonton.

Hunsperger began with a reference to Lady Gaga's paean to self-expression, "Born This Way," released in 2011. Hunsperger begged to differ:

> The world is believing the lie that because you were "born this way" you now have a right to live this way – the way you were born. Sounds great at first except nobody is mentioning what the results will be of living the way you were born! If you were "born this way," are you going to "die this way?" Well if that is true, and it is, then you have fallen right into the trap that is as old as time. That trap is what satan wants for you – but is that what you want? You see, you can live the way you were born, and if you die the way you were born

then you will suffer the rest of eternity in the lake of fire, hell, a place of eternal suffering.

He then drew a specific gay connection by making a reference to the Edmonton Public Schools inclusiveness policy:

The Board is committed to establishing and maintaining a safe, inclusive, equitable, and welcoming learning and teaching environment for all members of the school community. This includes those students, staff, and families who identify or are perceived as lesbian, gay, bisexual, transgender, transsexual, two-spirit, queer or questioning their sexual orientation, gender identity, or gender expression. The Board expects all members of our diverse community to be welcomed, respected, accepted, and supported in every school.

From there he went on to tell a story about a personal encounter with a couple of gay men:

Our family was flying from California back to Calgary and we had to make a change over in San Francisco. As we were waiting for our plane to leave, two men who were homosexuals were also waiting and we began to share in conversation. Once they found out that I was a pastor the conversation went to their lifestyle and they began to expand how we as Christians have judged them wrongly. Then one of the men said to me, "You will never understand

what it is like to be born one way and have society expect
to you live another."

This, Hunsperger said, was a moment of revelation for him:

Immediately Holy Spirit dropped this in my mouth and I
said, "You know, I do understand, because I was born the
same way. I was born living one way and God expects me to
live another way. I can't do that on my own and that's why
Jesus Christ came so I could be changed." Warning people to
not live the way they were born is not judgment or condemnation – it is love! Accepting people the way they are is cruel
and not loving!

Evaluated as a piece of public speaking, this was a pretty
good sermon. It combined a personal anecdote with a reference to pop culture (Lady Gaga), public policy (Edmonton
schools), and vivid imagery from the Book of Revelation (lake
of fire). But it was politically lethal because it expressed the
view that gay sexuality was a sinful condition to be overcome
through religious conversion. Even though all Christian
churches and sects, as well as other religions, taught this fifty
years ago, and some still do, you can't publicly support this
position and expect to be active in Canadian politics today.

Because Hunsperger's sermon was posted on his church's
website rather than his own, Wildrose had missed the post in
its research on its own candidates, but the Progressive Conservatives found it and tipped the media to it at the beginning of

the final week. The "lake of fire" episode proved to be the turning point in the campaign, in part because Smith refused to perform human sacrifice on the Reverend Hunsperger. She condemned Hunsperger's homophobic sentiments but did not take the further step of saying that Hunsperger, if elected, would not be allowed to sit in the Wildrose caucus (under election law, it was too late for the party to withdraw his nomination). Senior members of the campaign team had recommended that Smith take that further step; but she had some good reasons for her decision, and as campaign manager I defended her within the party against those who thought she should have acted differently. But she was widely criticized for having seemed weak, and afterwards decided that she must appear more resolute in the future. Thus I became the human sacrifice that she had not performed in April 2012. Her action would have made more sense if I had actually said that I was "okay with child pornography," but she was obviously so spooked by what she had not done in 2012 that, with Redford already out ahead of her in the news cycle, she could not take time for a little research and reflection in 2013.

Denunciation by the Prime Minister's Office was also prompted by short-term political considerations. A person I know in the PMO told me afterwards that their phones were "melting down" after the YouTube video was posted, and that they had to distance themselves from the words *no harm* that I had used in my abortive attempt to explain what I had meant. The rationale is familiar: react to the inflammatory phrase taken out of context, respond immediately, don't worry about collateral damage to people. So the director of communications was told to tweet something.

Behind this standard rapid-response strategy lie longer-term political factors. Conservative political parties in Canada have been trading heavily on child pornography for two decades, ever since Brian Mulroney's government introduced the first legislation in 1993. Stephen Harper's Conservative government had brought in legislation to increase mandatory minimum prison sentences for mere possession as recently as 2012. On at least three occasions, conservative politicians or campaign organizations have tried to label opponents as supporters of child pornography – Stockwell Day against Lorne Goddard in 1999; the Conservative war room against Liberal prime minister Paul Martin in the 2004 federal election campaign; and Minister of Public Safety Vic Toews against opponents of his draft Internet surveillance legislation in 2012. Conservative parties in general, and Stephen Harper's government in particular, have invested heavily in prolonging the 1980s moral panic over child pornography. They thus must have felt politically endangered when I, who had been close to the prime minister in the past, was quoted, even out of context, as being tolerant of child pornography.

It must also be said that Prime Minister Harper has made a practice of treating people as disposable, regardless of previous contributions to him and the Conservative Party. For instance, in 2007, when Brian Mulroney's dealings with Karl-Heinz Schreiber were in the news, Harper told the entire Conservative caucus not to talk to the former prime minister. Someone in the organization also leaked to the media the fact that Mulroney's party membership was not up to date. I'd call it pretty harsh treatment for a former Conservative prime minister who had been actively supporting Harper in the media and behind the scenes. I was in Harper's office on the morning of May 17, 2005, when we learned that Belinda Stronach had crossed the floor to join the Liberals. The phone rang within an hour; it was Brian Mulroney, calling from his hospital bed to cheer Harper up. Mulroney had almost died that spring of pancreatitis, but he still thought to console Harper in his time of trial. In my opinion, that should have counted for something in 2007. Harper had to distance himself at that time because of Mulroney's legal problems, but he didn't have to go out of his way to humiliate the former prime minister.

The list of Harper's disposable people grows steadily. Some of the more prominent names would include Helena Guergis, who was forced out of Cabinet and caucus on reports of drug abuse that were never substantiated; Senators Mike Duffy, Pamela Wallin, and Patrick Brazeau, who were suspended from the Conservative caucus and the Senate over allegedly dodgy expense claims; and Chief of Staff Nigel Wright, who was left to take all the blame for writing a cheque for $90,000 to Mike Duffy. So I can count myself in pretty good company among those who have been crushed by Harper's PMO.

To some extent, this is a reflection of the shadow side of Harper's personality, but it is also a cancer eating at the whole conservative movement in Canada, and I have to accept my share of blame for it. When the Liberals seemed to be in power forever, Conservatives concluded that part of their secret of success was ruthlessness. Under Jean Chrétien, the Liberals never hesitated to smear opponents, run negative ads, cancel embarrassing inquiries, and in general play political hardball. We concluded that we would have to beat them at their own game, and we did. Harper led the way, but everyone around him bought into it, and then the doctrine of ruthlessness sifted down into provincial conservative parties wanting to emulate the success of the federal party.

Aristotle said virtue is in the mean. I'm still trying to figure out where the mean is on this issue. Politics is a tough business, and you can't win elections and run governments without being thick-skinned and hard-headed. Yet something is wrong when people become disposable simply for being inconvenient. On my last appearance with Evan Solomon on *Power and Politics*, I joked that I was the Trotsky of the Canadian conservative movement. The ice pick came far faster than I expected. But did Trotsky have a right to complain about the ice pick, given his crucial role in bringing the Bolsheviks to power? Good question for a seminar on ethics and politics.

Preston Manning, another political leader for whom I once worked, also denounced me that morning. His reasons were somewhat different. He is no longer in active politics and has never had any particular connection with the issue of child pornography. However, his Manning Centre has become a major promoter of the concept of a "conservative movement" in Canada. The centre was scheduled to hold its annual networking conference in March, and I was supposed to participate in a panel on Aboriginal economic progress along with Manny Jules and other native leaders. As Preston later told me, when the Incident broke in the media, he and his advisers were afraid that my presence at the conference would attract too much attention and thus derail the conference from its larger purpose. I agree with that analysis and would gladly have stepped back from the program if requested. That the Manning Centre felt it necessary to denounce me publicly without attempting first to deal with the problem in the more usual and private way is evidence of how powerfully the combination of moral panic and short media cycle affects behaviour.

Preston, however, showed his true character by apologizing to me a few weeks afterwards. In an email sent on Good Friday, a significant day to a man of Preston's deep Christian faith, he admitted that the Manning Centre had acted too hastily, and he offered to take public steps to help restore my reputation. Truly moved by his initiative, I responded that I had made so many mistakes in my own life that I had no right to hold a grudge. Thus far, Preston Manning is the only person from the political world who has offered an apology. He still stands out, as he always has, as a man of character in our often shoddy political scene.

By the time I reached my office in Calgary shortly before noon on February 28, I had been condemned by the prime minister of Canada through his director of communications and personally by the premier of Alberta, the leader of the Wildrose Party, and the former leader of the Reform Party. The list included all the politicians for whom I had ever worked. These public condemnations inevitably signalled days of media swarming. News stories, unsigned editorials, and op-ed pieces followed for ten days of media hell. Most of the leading pundits in the country stayed away from it; perhaps they could see themselves one day also becoming folk devils. But the story was now sitting there for journeymen reporters and second-tier columnists to exploit – unacceptable remarks plus universal condemnation by conservative leaders. Stir it all up and add a little tut-tutting – I was supposed to be smart, how could I be so stupid, and so on.

Taking a long view of history, maybe I should just shut up and count my blessings. While working on this chapter, I was also listening on my car CD player to Stacy Schiff's biography of the Egyptian queen, Cleopatra. In her era, the penalty for getting on the wrong side of political leaders was quick death by the sword if you were lucky, slow death by gruesome torture if you were unlucky. Neither Cleopatra nor any of her playmates, such as Julius Caesar, Marc Antony, and Octavian, had the slightest respect for human life. All I suffered was verbal condemnation followed by a media mobbing, with concomitant loss of reputation. And yet we are fortunate enough to live in a gentler age, when rights are supposed to include more than mere physical safety, supremely important though that is. If we are serious about the protection of rights such as freedom of speech, we have to think about the many ways other than death, torture, and imprisonment that politicians can intimidate those over whom they rule.

## Public and Private

At this point an interesting and important pattern started to emerge. Public-sector organizations continued to pile on while I started to attract some sympathy and support from persons and organizations in the private sector. As I mentioned, the most prominent public actor was the CBC, which cancelled my *Power and Politics* contract. The CBC is one of the biggest media companies in Canada, with a very large staff for collecting, analyzing, and reporting the news. Yet it cancelled my contract and publicly denounced me on the basis of a single YouTube video, without asking for any input from me about the context of that video. It also declined to let me make the appearance that day for which I had been previously scheduled and at which I could have explained what had happened. Moral panic and the excitement of mobbing triumphed over all normal canons of journalism because folk devils have no right to speak. And then came another public piling-on I described earlier: my own university's press release, implying that I was tolerant of child pornography and that I was being pushed into retirement because of my opinions, which I discuss at greater length in the chapter on academic freedom.

Behind the scenes, other universities also behaved with great haste and little seeming regard for academic freedom. York University immediately cancelled an invitation for me to debate the former clerk of the Privy Council, Alex Himmelfarb, on whether taxes in Canada should be increased. Brigham

Young University in Provo, Utah, rescinded an invitation to speak on Canadian political parties as part of its annual Canada Week (my numerous Mormon in-laws say they still love me, even though BYU looms in their imaginations the same way that Notre Dame does for Catholics). Montreal's Concordia University did, however, act with more deliberation and finally decided to uphold its invitation to be part of its annual Workshops on Social Science Research. I'm grateful to my former student Mebs Kanji, who teaches there and who had originally arranged the invitation, for deterring Concordia from joining the rush to judgment.

Other public-sector organizations behaved in similar fashion. An invitation to address the annual meeting of chief electoral officers was summarily cancelled. The journal *Policy Options* quickly withdrew its offer to publish an article I had written (at their request) on the 2012 Calgary Centre by-election campaign. *Policy Options* is sponsored by the Montreal-based Institute for Research on Public Policy, which accepts government financial support. In contrast, the Fraser Institute, which does not accept government money, took time to deliberate and then affirmed my status as a senior fellow.

The new British consul-general in Calgary provided a comical example of public-sector aversion to risk. Though I had never met him, he had been emailing me for weeks for a meeting to talk about politics in Canada and Alberta. I've often done this for diplomatic representatives from the United States, Japan, and other countries, so I was happy to set up a time. Shortly after the Incident, I got an email from him that our meeting was cancelled, and I haven't heard from him since. Now I was a diplomatic *persona non grata*.

In contrast, I received a lot of support from people in the private sector – academic colleagues, past and present students, readers of my publications, and many people who just care about fair play. I've already mentioned the hundreds of emails, phone calls, and letters that came to me expressing various degrees of sympathy or support for my position. These were crucial in helping me get through such a difficult time. Human beings are social beings, so when you're being condemned on all sides, you can hardly survive without some other sources of emotional support. Family members can do a lot, but they are also victims along with you. You need to hear from friends and people you've never met and who may not even agree with you but who are repelled by mobbing and who support freedom of speech.

It was striking that almost all the expressions of support I got came from people outside of government. After more than twenty years playing politics, I know a lot of people in public life – judges, senators, MPs, provincial politicians, civil servants, political party staff – and many other people in public life would probably recognize my name from my media appearances. Yet I did not hear from more than a handful of this vast number of people. They may have feared that a sympathetic email might get publicized and cause them embarrassment; indeed, a few political people later spoke to me in person when I bumped into them at social occasions. But I suspect that most have become inured to the practice of human sacrifice, which has become so prevalent in our age of gotcha politics.

Also striking was the contrast of the behaviour of private-sector media with that of the public-sector CBC. As I mentioned, *The Globe and* Mail offered to continue the monthly column that I have been writing since 2006, the *National Post* volunteered to give me space for a column, and *Maclean's Magazine* arranged a feature interview with Anne Kingston.

Of course, patterns of this type are never perfectly consistent. While the public-sector TVO gave me a chance to explain myself on Steve Paikin's *The Agenda*, the private-sector *Sun* newspapers, whose populism often borders on demagoguery, were particularly brutal in their reporting of the Incident. So the pattern was not perfect, but it was certainly there.

Also significant is that within two weeks of the Incident, Doug Pepper, publisher at Signal/McClellland & Stewart (an imprint of Random House of Canada), got in touch to discuss publishing a book. Signal/M&S has published other controversial Canadian authors, such as Conrad Black and Ezra Levant, yet it is a commercial enterprise that has to make money on the books it publishes. It's a perfect illustration of the importance of the profit motive in preserving freedom of speech. People holding unpopular ideas that challenge conventional wisdom may be shouted down by politicians and government agencies, but they may still get a hearing if they can find a private patron. Where would Marx have been without the industrialist Engels to support him? But Marx was dependent on Engels's goodwill and ideological commitment, whereas the profit motive can lead to publication even if the publisher doesn't care about, or even dislikes, an author's views. The result is this book, *Persona Non Grata*.

In contemporary Canada, we often speak as if the primary guarantee of freedom of expression is section 2 of the Canadian Charter of Rights and Freedoms, adopted in 1982:

> 2. Everyone has the following fundamental freedoms:
> (*a*) freedom of conscience and religion;
> (*b*) freedom of thought, belief, opinion and expression, including freedom of the press and other media of communication;
> (*c*) freedom of peaceful assembly; and
> (*d*) freedom of association.

It's great to have Charter protection of free speech, yet Canadians enjoyed that freedom long before the Charter was adopted. It was protected by our constitutional tradition of the rule of law, which tries sets limits on arbitrary action by governments.

The rule of law, in turn, is important because it protects the property and contractual rights of citizens. We normally (and correctly) think of property and contract as the basis of the market economy, but they also provide the infrastructure for all forms of freedom of expression. For freedom of religion to have genuine meaning, believers have to be able to build, buy, or rent space to worship together. The same is true for freedom of assembly; people need space to hold political meetings. Let's apply that logic to freedom of speech.

Expressing ideas in our large societies means more than the right to hold a private conversation with friends. It means to the right to look for means of publication in order to reach larger audiences – to publish a book, set up a website, place an ad on TV or in the newspapers, put up billboards, send out direct mail, and many other activities – all of which are essentially economic transactions and thus depend on ownership of property and enforcement of contractual agreements in order to take place. Freedom of speech also requires some protection of those economic rights that underpin our livelihood. Most people will not take a chance expressing unpopular ideas if the predictable result is losing their job or their home.

Picture a society where the state owns all the "means of production." It's not that hard to imagine: just think of the Soviet Union before 1990. Then picture an annoying writer, call him Dr. Tom, who has ideas of which the regime does not approve. How will he publish them? The state owns all the publishing companies, media outlets, and computer networks. If he self-publishes (*samizdat*) with, say, a photocopier, how long will he be able to hold on to his job or the place where he lives?

The role of labour unions and professional organizations should also be factored into the analysis. Most people in modern societies are economically dependent upon the jobs that they hold to provide a flow of income. They may own some property – house, savings, investments – but not enough to support them for more than a few months without income from paid employment. Holding a job is not a property right, a right of ownership, but it is associated with personal rights set forth in the common and statutory law of contract, as well as in the provisions of collective agreements, where such exist. In a free society, unions and professional associations perform an invaluable service by helping to defend the legal employments rights of their members. Without the academic freedom and tenure clauses of the collective agreement under which I was working at the University of Calgary, and without the Faculty Association to defend them, the university could have terminated my services or otherwise engaged in reprisals against me for what I had reportedly said. So it is not only private property that protects freedom of speech but also the larger context of the rule of law.

Considerations of this type were highly relevant in my case. My question about the appropriate punishment for simple possession of child pornography displeased some of the most powerful politicians in the country, including the prime minister of Canada and the premier of Alberta. The CBC – the state-owned broadcaster – immediately cancelled my contract. I was only able to continue communicating with the public because Canada is also graced with media outlets – newspapers, magazines, publishing houses – not owned by the state. Moreover, important politicians, including Thomas Lukaszuk, Alberta's minister of advanced education, and James Moore, Canada's minister of Canadian heritage, called upon the University of Calgary to fire me. My own university, rather than protesting at such political pressure, issued a press release implying that I was being pushed into retirement. How long would my job have been safe if I had not had a contract of employment enforceable in independent courts of law?

Those on the left in Canada – liberals and social democrats – tend to favour Charter rights such as freedom of expression, but they are often dismissive of economic rights such as property and contract. Those on the right – conservatives – see the importance of economic rights but are sometimes ready to repress dissent. Both sides need to recognize that the two sides of freedom – economic and expressive – are mutually dependent. Neither will survive very long unless both are protected. This isn't a new insight; Hayek made the same point decades ago. But it remains as important as ever.

CHAPTER 5

# THE END OF PRIVACY

▲

## The Rise of New Media

A CENTRAL FEATURE OF THE INCIDENT WAS THE
dramatic acceleration of the news cycle that has occurred in
recent decades. Twenty years ago, what happened to me
simply could not have happened, at least not in the way it did.
To see why, let's dredge up some old memories.

When I went to work for Preston Manning in May 1991,
one of my first jobs was to clean up several months of correspondence that had built up in his office. I spent three weeks
dictating replies into a Dictaphone, replies that were then typed
by an administrative assistant. The Internet and email may have
existed as developmental prototypes, but they were not available in the Reform Party office, or anywhere else in my world.

Ditto for cellphones. Remember the clunky portable phones
that Jerry Seinfeld and his friends used in their apartments? They
were state of the art for the early 1990s. The first cellphone did

not appear in a *Seinfeld* episode until 1996. Photographic technology was equally primitive; the Polaroid camera appeared in more than one *Seinfeld* episode. In the famous next-to-last episode (1998), the group used a bulky camcorder, not a mobile phone, to record a robbery and carjacking.

As a mental experiment, try to imagine what it would have been like if I had been asked to speak on the Indian Act at the University of Lethbridge twenty years previously, at 7 p.m., Wednesday, February 24, 1993. There would have been no media present; reporters don't normally cover evening events because it is too late to file for the evening television news or the morning edition of the newspaper. Maybe, as also happened in 2013, a reporter for the *Lethbridge Herald* would have done an advance interview about what I planned to say so he could file a story for the next day's paper. Depending on the judgment of the editor, that might have led to a published story on the Indian Act but nothing about child pornography.

Without the Internet, no one in the audience would have known that once in my career I had made a two-sentence sidebar statement about child pornography. What happened in 2009 in Winnipeg would have stayed in Winnipeg. The recording of my Winnipeg speech, made with my permission, and the resulting article in the student newspaper might have ended up in the opposition files of federal political parties, but there is little chance they would have given it to Levi Little Mustache for an ambush in Lethbridge. By 2013 I had been out of federal politics for seven years and was no longer worth a direct attack.

My presentation twenty years ago might have been audio recorded with my permission, as happened in Winnipeg. It could have been video recorded too, though that is less likely because equipment then was cumbersome and needed a technician to operate. But there was not much of an Internet then, and no YouTube or other means of instant publication. Even if I had said something outrageous, whoever recorded it, in whatever format, would have had to take it to a newspaper, or a radio or TV station. If a reporter had taken an interest in it, he probably would have had to call me to confirm what I had said, and I would have had a chance to insert my side of the story from the beginning. If anything ever did appear in the media, several days would have passed, maybe even a week or more. It would not have been a bombshell story. What would have been the headline? "Professor makes outrageous-sounding statement, but after he explained it, it sounded like normal classroom stuff"?

Even if a national dimension to the story had developed, it would have been far from instantaneous. Reporters would have to call the press officer of a political leader and try to schedule an interview, or at least leave a question for a call-back answer. Political staff would have tried to find out what was happening. Politicians, or their staff, couldn't make flash statements by email or Twitter. There would have been no Twitter to allow the prime minister's communications director to instantly convert an Alberta story into a front-page national story. There would have been time for everyone to think.

All the important events in my mobbing happened in the two and a half hours it took me to drive from Lethbridge to

Calgary on February 28; in fact, the main damage was done in the first hour. What happened to me was an instantaneous virtual mobbing, conducted at the speed of light through electronic media. Nobody actually did anything except look at images on screens, tap keys, and converse via telephone. No one threw stones at me, or hit and kicked me; no one approached me physically at all. But a virtual mobbing can be as dangerous to your reputation as a physical mobbing can be to your health.

Several technical advances of the last two decades have come together to make virtual mobbing possible. First is the invention of the Internet as an infinite electronic archive of everything published or spoken in public. The existence of the Internet furnishes far more, and more readily available, weapons for mobbing than ever existed in the days when research had to be physically conducted in libraries, archives, and newspaper morgues. Second is the invention of small digital recording devices, for both audio and video, which need no special expertise to operate. This means that anything can be recorded, anytime, anywhere. Third is the emergence of YouTube and other forms of social media, which allow instant publication of text and images without any editorial filtering by third parties. Now you can be your own publisher, without interference by nagging editors, fact-checkers, or referees. Fourth is the velocity of messaging via cellphone, email, texting, and social media platforms, all of which come together in the smartphone. The media can ask questions and politicians can give answers in seconds or minutes rather than days or weeks. Both questions and answers may be extremely superficial, generated with almost no time to think, but they immediately become part of the public record.

These technological innovations were crucial to the Incident. It would never have happened unless my 2009 sidebar comment on child pornography had been archived on the Internet. It also could not have happened without recording technology to capture my statement in Lethbridge without informing me that recording was taking place. The existence of YouTube allowed the video to be posted quickly and anonymously with a misleading tagline, which set the tone for mainstream media coverage. And Twitter allowed the prime minister's director of communications to send the story into overdrive by tapping a few keys. With these four technological innovations, new media became the trigger for a mainstream media massacre.

An important result of these developments is that there are no longer any reliably private discussions, conversations, or even moments. Any sound or image can be recorded. It is now so easy that there is no point trying to prevent it. Anyone can have a cellphone turned on at any time, and there is no way to stop it except by universal body searches. In 2009, *The Manitoban* reporter asked permission to record my lecture, but that seems quaintly old-fashioned in 2013. Arnell Tailfeathers didn't ask my permission, or even give me notice, that he was recording the Lethbridge event in 2013; it probably never occurred to him to ask. Not all discussions or conversations *will* be recorded, but they all *could* be recorded. Previously, someone who wanted to keep things private might resort to a private meeting or a phone call rather than send a letter that could be photocopied or an email that could be forwarded. But that kind of guarantee of privacy is rapidly coming to an end. We are quickly approaching Marshall McLuhan's global village. Because it is so huge, we can't say that everyone will know everything about everyone; but with a little effort, anyone will be able to learn anything about anyone.

Instant publication on social media portals is also highly relevant in this connection. The public seems to regard recordings, especially video recordings, as *ipso facto* true, the highest evidence of what actually took place, history *wie es eigentlich gewesen,* as Leopold von Ranke said. That may have made some sense when cumbersome equipment had to be operated by technicians and news organizations took responsibility for editing recordings and putting them in comprehensible context. But on YouTube there is no context, merely raw footage and text. In my case, that meant posting an audiovisual record of a couple of minutes out of a two-and-a-half-hour event, under a tendentious tagline not reviewed by any editor: "Tom Flanagan okay with child pornography." The title did not fairly express either what I had said or what I think, but it quickly became the basis of countless headlines on websites, print pages, and news broadcasts.

It's a bit like what happened to the main character in Tom Wolfe's latest novel *Back to Blood*. Nestor, a Cuban American cop in Miami, has to take down a much larger black drug offender. Someone posts a video of the end of the violent encounter without including the whole series of actions, and

Nestor is suspended from active duty amid charges of racial prejudice. By now, any reasonably well-informed observer of the news should be highly suspicious of videos posted by interested parties without full disclosure of the context.

To the casual consumer of the news, it must have seemed as if I had decided to make a public statement of my views about child pornography, and the proof was the recording. But in fact I hadn't made a statement. I had been asked a question, and I tried to respond by asking another question, as a way of getting people to think about the issue. I wasn't trying to address the public at large. I mistakenly thought I was engaged in a dialectical enterprise with an audience in which we could reason together. It wasn't private in the narrow sense of a conversation among a small number of people, but it was, at least in my intention, a collective undertaking among the people in the room. Publishing a recorded snippet without any context stripped the moment of its meaning and turned it into a public factoid that severely misrepresented what had happened in the room that night. This kind of "publication" means the end of privacy for any teacher or presenter or group leader who tries to reason or work with a group of people. What football coach or artistic director or platoon leader or choreographer could survive if all his or her shouted or whispered instructions were subject to being posted on the web at any moment?

Making a presentation to an audience is part of the same genre of human events, particularly when Q&A is included. It's not just showing PowerPoint. It's a dialectical process that tries to help audience members discover conclusions, conclusions that may be quite different for different people. Appearance, demeanour, body language, anecdotes, jokes, and banter are all part of it. That's why people come to live events. If it were just a matter of looking at PowerPoint, we might as well stay home and watch in comfort. But people come to be part of an event constructed for those who take the trouble to attend. Invasion through secret recording and publication destroys the semi-private sense of togetherness necessary to make a presentation truly memorable. If both presenter and audience have to be constantly on guard about everything they say, it's the end of privacy and the end of intellectual adventure.

Another assault on privacy comes from the Internet's role as infinite archive of memory. French scholar Ernest Renan said that "the essence of a nation is, that all its individual members should have many things in common; and also that all of them should hold many things in oblivion." What is true of national identity is also true of personal identity. Individual identity is not an unchanging essence; it is continuously updated and renegotiated as individuals sally forth to meet the new day's events. Maybe no one can or should have complete control over his own identity, but individuals will lose the ability even to influence their definition of self if nothing is ever forgotten. If everything you've ever written or said is archived and readily accessible and liable to be thrown back at you at any time, you have no privacy as an individual presenting yourself to others. If everything is eternally public and nothing can be forgotten, individuals lose all private control over their own identity.

The situation is even worse than what I have just described because what the Internet "remembers" is always partial, often distorted, and sometimes completely false. As a story breaks on social media and is then reported in the mainstream news, a stylized version quickly emerges. Certain facts are repeated over and over, while others slip into oblivion. Remarks of commentators are woven into the story as if they were part of the factual record, not comments about it. The end result is a standardized media narrative, sitting on many places on the Internet. Whenever a journalist wants to do a new story about an issue, the first step is a quick Internet search, which is bound to turn up the standardized media narrative. The journalist copies it into a story template, then adds whatever new factoid seems to justify a new story. If the story has any legs, he may do follow-up articles, each time preserving the standardized media narrative while piling new factoids on top.

None of this takes much time, effort, or thought, which is an excellent thing from the perspective of news organizations. The rise of new media has put the traditional media – newspapers, radio, and TV – under extreme economic pressure. Venerable print outlets have cut back their number of press runs, transformed themselves into e-zines, or ceased publication altogether. Survivors have drastically pruned staff, both at the reporting and editorial level. The mainstream media could not report news today without the help of the Internet and all the stylized narratives archived on it.

As an example of how this works, consider what happened in Calgary on May 10, 2013, when Conrad Black gave a luncheon presentation to a large business audience at the Petroleum Club. During the question-and-answer period, he happened to touch on my case, saying that I had made a "perfectly reasonable point" in Lethbridge. Black was sensitive to the issue because, as he explained in his recent book *A Matter of Principle,* he had met in American prisons men who were serving long terms for viewing child pornography. In fact, at one time his cellmate was a bisexual Boston chef who had been convicted of that offence.

The *Calgary Herald* reported some of what Black said but also drew on the standard media narrative to characterize what I had said: "Tom Flanagan got into hot water for comments he made at the University of Lethbridge suggesting child pornography didn't cause harm and questioning whether people who view those images should be jailed." But I never said that child pornography didn't cause harm; I asked whether it was necessary to jail people whose only offence was to have looked at child pornography, if they hadn't themselves caused harm to children. Since discussion was cut off, I never got a chance to develop John Stuart Mill's distinction between direct and indirect harm. But what I actually said doesn't matter in news coverage; what counts is what is readily available in the Internet narrative.

Omission is a factor too. The story did not mention that the room broke into spontaneous applause in the wake of Black's comments. An event took place: a famous man made a comment about the Incident, and perhaps two hundred members of the Calgary business community responded with a show of support for his remarks. But that didn't get reported, probably because it didn't fit into the standard narrative of how I had become a pariah and my career was over.

I don't think the *Herald*'s reporter intended to write a hostile article; in fact, he was kind enough to let me add a little comment afterwards. My point is that he couldn't help himself from relying on the standard narrative. Distorted factoids from the Internet archive get repeated, while new facts that don't fit the model aren't reported. On to the next story!

Yet a third way in which privacy is threatened is by the weakness of the isolated individual facing the media-Internet behemoth. Now, as it happened, I was peculiarly defenceless when my story broke. I was driving from Lethbridge to Calgary, and I did not even have a cellphone with me (I did have a car phone, but almost no one has the number). I own a primitive cellphone, but I rarely have it with me unless I'm on a lengthier trip and will have to contact people. The fact is that I generally don't like people to be able to call me at their pleasure. My life has depended on having things to say and write, and I need privacy and solitude to think. It's not quite as strong as *cogito ergo sum,* but if I did not have time to think, I would have nothing worth saying or writing. I look forward to periods of solitude like the car trip back and forth to Lethbridge, when I can listen to an audiobook on the CD player to keep me awake and let part of my mind chew over whatever topics I'm working on.

I did have my iPad with me, but I have never set up any of my computers to automatically feed me whatever people are saying about me on the Internet. To be honest, I don't really care. Most of what's said on Twitter or Facebook or blog sites or chat lines, or even in published media stories, is ephemeral at best. I can't obsess about what people say about me if I'm to have anything of my own worth saying. I have to be able to focus on the topics on which I hope to communicate.

So you can say I was the author of my own misfortune. I certainly wasn't at the top of my media game, travelling without a cellphone and not monitoring what was being said about me on the Internet. But that's the whole point. I was a private person, invited because of my past writings to give a talk to a particular audience. I wasn't working for a political party or any other organization that takes collective positions. I was just a private person who other people thought might have something interesting to say. I didn't want to play the media game. I wanted to drive and think, and talk, and then drive and think some more.

Of course, it was completely different when I managed political campaigns. In those years, I had one or two cell-phones with me at all times, and I had an organization to monitor the media and alert me immediately if problems arose. I wasn't the public spokesman for an organization, but I was responsible for making sure that our spokesmen did their job and got it right, so I sacrificed my privacy out of necessity for doing my own job. But that was then and this was now.

Moreover, even if I had been travelling with the smartest of smartphones set up to feed me everything anyone in the world was saying about me on any platform, I would have been over-whelmed. Maybe a media genius like my former student Ezra

Levant could have survived, but I certainly couldn't. Most people, and that includes me, can't think clearly when dozens of people are trying to call you and hundreds, maybe thousands, of people are saying things about you on the Internet. You need the help of an organization to get through it, which is why leaders of major political parties have dozens of people working for them. In this kind of crisis, you need staff to intercept calls, track the media, brainstorm about responses, and present you with strategic alternatives. You would be committing reputational suicide to try to improvise, to deal with it spontaneously and unassisted. Political leaders, company presidents, and heads of organizations generally have that kind of organization to assist them, but the isolated individual is helpless in comparison.

Over the course of a few days, I was able to regroup. Friends came to my rescue with good advice and opportunities to tell my own story in my own way. I was lucky in that respect. Yet what happens if you have few friends, or if you have done something that drives your friends away? My only wrongdoing was to try to reason with an angry mob the way I would reason with a classroom of students, and my friends could recognize that. In the end, friends substituted for organization, for which I will always be grateful. But not everyone can count on that.

Alexis de Tocqueville wrote in *Democracy in America:*

Individuals in democracies are very weak, but the state, which represents them all and holds them all in the palm of its hand, is very strong. Nowhere else do the citizens seem smaller than in a democratic nation, and nowhere does the nation itself seem greater, so that it is easily conceived as a vast picture. Imagination shrinks at the thought of themselves as individuals and expands beyond all limits at the thought of the state.

When Tocqueville wrote these words, he had in mind the colossal scale of democratic monuments, evident even then in the layout of Washington, D.C. But if Tocqueville were alive today, he might apply that same line of thought to the relationship between the individual and the modern media. *Media* is properly a plural noun (one medium, many media), but we have come to use *the media* as a singular noun because we see it as a power beyond anyone's control. There is no secret, conspiratorial power behind the scenes directing the media, no Wizard of Oz behind a green curtain. What we call *media* is a set of institutions and incentives that lead participants to behave in certain ways, regardless of their intentions.

As technology has sped up the media cycle, it has created the potential for instantaneous virtual mobbing. Reporters work almost entirely by putting together what they read on the Internet with whatever comments they can glean by telephone or email. Newspapers as well as TV and radio stations all have their own websites. Important stories are posted on the Internet long before the evening news broadcast or tomorrow morning's print edition. Editors are under pressure to approve stories because there are so many competitors who are about to update their own websites. Media outlets no longer compete with other outlets in the same medium in a geographically defined market. All media outlets compete with one another, as well as with bloggers and social media platforms, to break stories. At one time, common sense would have said that a video unilaterally posted on YouTube is not sufficient basis for a story without further research, but that's no longer true in our steroidal news cycle.

In May 2013, *CBS Evening News* anchor Scott Pelley spoke about the media speed-up. Pelley is one of the most respected figures in American media today; in Canadian terms, this would be like a statement from Peter Mansbridge. It certainly is worthy of serious consideration:

> Never before in human history has more information been available to more people. But at the same time, never before in human history has more bad information been available to more people. . . .
>
> In a world where everyone is a publisher, no one is an editor. And that is the danger that we face today.
>
> We have entered a time when a writer's first idea is his best idea, when the first thing a reporter hears is the first thing that she reports. We live in a time now when we have seen major television networks take video off of YouTube and broadcast it to millions of Americans without verifying whether the video had been fabricated or not. Twitter, Facebook, and Reddit. That's not journalism. That's gossip. Journalism was invented as an antidote to gossip. . . .
>
> If you're first, no one will ever remember. If you're wrong, no one will ever forget.

How does it serve the public to be first in this frantic effort that we so often see that we all succumb to? How does it serve the public if we're first?

In the case of my Incident, Twitter played a crucial role in accelerating the pace of the story. The Prime Minister's Office chose to make an early statement by Twitter, meaning that someone speaking for the most powerful person in the country, someone for whom I had once been chief of staff, had denounced me within an hour of the story coming to public notice. That was a powerful signal across the country for others to pile on. Without the social medium of Twitter, the PMO could never have responded so quickly, and the mobbing would not have gathered steam in such a rush.

News is now more widely available than ever, and that's a good thing. New voices can make themselves heard without being blocked by media filters. But the technical progress and enhanced competition has also created new perils, such as instantaneous virtual mobbing, that we have to be aware of. What's to be done about all this? I can't claim to know, though I will make a few suggestions in the last chapter. I'm certainly not calling for government intervention; government is the biggest threat of all, as we saw in the preceding chapter. Maybe the market itself will evolve means for individuals to protect themselves. Maybe such means already exist for people more media-savvy than I, and it's just a matter of making them more usable to ordinary citizens. In the meantime, though, it would help if people in the media could slow down enough to ask themselves basic questions, such as, "Does it make sense to condemn someone who's been in public life for more than twenty years on the basis of one YouTube video to which he has had no chance to respond?"

To return to the theme of privacy, the underlying cause of my mobbing was that, after years of playing politics behind the scenes but at a high level, I tried to return to the private life of a university academic and occasional commentator on public affairs. Arnell Tailfeathers, Levi Little Mustache, and other Idle No More activists deployed political tactics against me when I thought I was acting as a private citizen. I thought I was expressing views in an ongoing debate over public policy, whereas they saw me as a political actor thwarting their ambitions for change. When I was a campaign manager, I authorized our operatives to tape political rallies put on by other parties in hopes that something would come up that we could use later. They were doing it to us, and they would not be surprised that we were doing it to them. But that's the point – we were doing it to each other, playing the political game. We were not ambushing private citizens.

Some political friends whom I greatly respect have suggested to me that it is simply not possible in Canada to become a purely private citizen again after having worked at a high level for a political leader. One friend, who has experienced some ups and downs in his own life, wrote to me:

When you play in the political world at the highest levels, you simply cannot inhabit both (to use your words) the "academic" and "non-academic life" so long as the politicians you have worked for remain in power or in leadership positions. Everything you do reflects on them. Everything. Everything. Everything. And everything you do is fair game for them (and others) to comment on or react to. That is the price we pay for having influence and senior positions of authority in politics. There is no statute of limitations for senior political advisors other than the defeat or dismissal of those advised.

After reading this advice, I understand better why the Liberals used to use Question Period to badger Prime Minister Harper about things I had said or written, even though I had stopped working for him in 2005. At the time, I just thought it was comical, even if annoying to the prime minister, but it illustrates what my friend was trying to say. Canadian politics can be like the Hotel California: you can check out, but you can never leave.

Maybe that's the way it has to be, though it's worth noting that the friends who have advanced this proposition to me work somewhere in the government relations industry as lobbyists, communications advisers, or strategists. Since their livelihood remains focused on serving people in government, it makes sense that they should keep their heads down and not expect to be perceived as independent individuals; they really haven't tried to check out of the Hotel California. But should the same norms apply to academics, researchers, and writers whose careers depend on being judged as individuals, not as supporters of a party or leader?

In the United States, academics and writers routinely move from their university or literary worlds into government, serving leaders of both parties, and then go back to their long-term homes and resume their careers as independent thinkers. Henry Kissinger became secretary of state for Republican Richard Nixon and later went back to Harvard. Lawrence Summers was secretary of the treasury for Democrat Bill Clinton, then also returned to Harvard. David Frum wrote speeches for a year for George W. Bush, then resumed his career as a writer and pundit. Barack Obama has a raft of academics around him who will do the same when their time in government is over.

In my case, I never had an ambition to work in government or government relations. I never wanted to be anything other than a university teacher, researcher, writer, and commentator on public affairs. Three times I accepted invitations from political leaders who thought I could help them by organizing their offices and running their political campaigns – Preston Manning in 1991, Stephen Harper in 2001, and Danielle Smith in 2012. I was too inexperienced to be of much use to Manning, I was for a few years an important asset to Harper, and I think I did a pretty fair job for Smith on short notice. But I would never have accepted any of these invitations if I had thought it entailed a long-term, perhaps lifetime obligation to give up my university and media career and work anonymously in government or government relations.

Maybe it has to be that way in Canada. Maybe our constitutional system of responsible Parliamentary government, which encourages the emergence of highly disciplined, secretive party organizations, means entry into politics has to be like checking into the Hotel California. It has, indeed, largely been that way in the past. But if that's the way it has to be, I would caution all academic colleagues against ever getting involved directly with politicians. If you want to have some influence on the decision-making processes of government, you can serve in various advisory capacities where you will be buffered from the political process itself. But if you get inside a political party, you may never be able to get out, at least not without incurring great costs to your reputation and financial position.

## CHAPTER 6

# ACADEMIC FREEDOM
# AND TEACHING

## Defending Academic Freedom

The Incident raised many questions not just about freedom of speech in general but also academic freedom in particular, both for professors and for students. What happened suggests that academic freedom is less securely protected in Canada than we might like to think.

Academic freedom is a set of privileges awarded to universities and colleges in light of their special mission: to seek and communicate knowledge about the universe, about human beings and societies, and about the cultures that are an integral part of human societies. An atmosphere of free inquiry is essential for verifying knowledge and passing it on. Raising questions about accepted truths is an integral part of the search process; and if those who raise such questions are made the target of reprisals, truth will be the loser. Falsehoods will go undetected, and truths will not be defended as well as they deserve to be if challenges are forestalled.

The Canadian Association of University Teachers (CAUT) describes academic freedom in these terms: "CAUT actively defends academic freedom as the the right to teach, learn, study and publish free of orthodoxy or threat of reprisal and discrimination. Academic freedom includes the right to criticize the university and the right to participate in its governance."

In itself, this is just a statement of desirability, without any legal force. The legal status of academic freedom in Canada comes from its insertion into collective agreements at universities and colleges. For example, the collective agreement between the University of Calgary and The University of Calgary Faculty Association (TUCFA) has this to say about academic freedom:

> The University is committed to the pursuit of truth and the advancement of learning as well as to the dissemination of knowledge. The Parties to this Agreement subscribe to the principles of academic freedom, that is, the right of the academic staff to examine, to question, to teach, to learn, to investigate, to speculate, to comment and to criticize without deference to prescribed doctrines, and recognize the right of academic staff to engage in these activities. Academic freedom includes the duty to use that freedom in a manner consistent with the responsibility to base research and teaching on an honest search for knowledge.

In Canada, academic freedom is not created and protected by legislation, but provincial legislation does establish the collective bargaining process for negotiating and enforcing collective agreements. In that sense, academic freedom has achieved standing in Canadian law.

The CAUT says, "Tenure provides a foundation for academic freedom by ensuring that academic staff cannot be dismissed without just cause and rigorous due process." Another phrase for tenure is "appointment with definite term," which staff members in modern universities receive as a reward for adequate performance after a probationary period of several years. Once that status is reached, the staff member can only be dismissed for just cause, such as professional incompetence or moral turpitude, objectively demonstrated to a neutral third party, such as an arbitration panel. If academic freedom is guaranteed in the collective agreement, expression of heterodox opinions cannot become just cause for dismissal.

The protection of academic freedom through tenure really amounts to defending professors from economic reprisals for expressing their views. The law of the land is already supposed to protect them from physical reprisals, such as imprisonment by the state or assaults by other citizens; tenure adds another layer of protection from the consequences of expressing their views in the process of searching for knowledge. Tenure means that the employer – the university administration – cannot fire professors, or force them into retirement, or reduce their salaries simply for what they may say or not say (silence is also protected). Many disputes have also established lesser but still important dimensions of academic freedom: professors may not be deprived of access to laboratories or libraries, or the opportunity to teach courses in their field, simply for opinions they have espoused.

Academic freedom institutionalized through tenure is a remarkable privilege that most citizens do not possess. In any line of work outside the university, you must reckon with the possibility of economic reprisals for what you say. If the government of the day decides to intervene in Syria, an air force general who gives a speech or writes a newspaper column to decry the folly of toppling one regime without thinking whether its successor might be even worse is headed for speedy retirement. The same would be true if the vice-president of marketing in a major oil company called for abandoning petroleum products in favour of wind and solar energy, or the director of nursing in a hospital denounced antibiotics in favour of homeopathic remedies; they would soon be looking for a new line of work.

Professors enjoy the great privilege of academic freedom only because their highest commitment is supposed to be not the advancement of their careers or the aggrandizement of their institutions (though they obviously do care about such things) but the search for verified knowledge and the communication of that knowledge to students and the public. The justification of academic freedom is utilitarian. It is granted because it is essential if science and scholarship are to function effectively; it is not an intrinsic right of the professorial caste.

The privilege of academic freedom is enormous but not absolute. Professors remain subject to the legal restrictions on speech that bind all citizens, such as laws against hate speech, defamation, sedition, and obscenity, giving rise to vexing practical questions. Is an anthropologist who studies human racial differences fomenting hatred against minority groups? Is the Islamist political scientist who expounds the grievances of the Muslim world against the West promoting acts of terrorism? Was it an artistic act of protest for a student to behead a live chicken in the college cafeteria? (The Alberta College of Art instructor who allegedly encouraged this piece of performance art was fired but then quickly reinstated.)

Professors receive the privilege of academic freedom not because they are such wonderful people but because a climate of free inquiry is essential to their work. Thus academic freedom does not protect everything any professor may say or do if it is not rationally connected to teaching and research. A physicist might use slides of famous paintings in his classes to illustrate something about the nature of colour, but the university would be justified in intervening if he turned his optics class into a course on art criticism. He would, however, be free to publicly expound his views on art without incurring penalties in his career as a physicist. It can get very complicated, which is why universities have review panels and arbitration proceedings and why particularly thorny questions of academic freedom sometimes require an answer from a court interpreting the collective agreement in the light of more general principles of Canadian law.

Historically, academic freedom in North America developed out of disputes not over such fine points but over reprisals directed at professors who publicly espoused dissident opinions challenging the conventional wisdom of the time. Such dissidents were usually on the radical "left," in one or another of the many meanings of that term – Marxists, communists, anarchists, atheists, or sexual libertines. Their utterances would provoke criticism from the university's board of directors, from major donors, or from governments providing financial support to the university, leading to discipline or even firing. But that sort of straightforward confrontation, which characterized the heroic age of academic freedom, has not been much in evidence in Canada in recent decades. Radical professors may still receive lots of criticism from the public, but they are unlikely to be fired for that alone. Current controversies are more likely to involve professors accused of sexual harassment, or of refusing to follow institutional policies on grading, or students who organize demonstrations to prevent visiting speakers from being heard on campus.

Though I am hardly a heroic figure, my Incident was a sort of throwback to the heroic age. While speaking in an academic setting on a university campus, I made a comment (actually, just asked a question) about public policy vis-à-vis the punishment for looking at child pornography. I was not venturing outside my discipline, advocating criminal behaviour, engaging in an obscene performance, or doing anything else other than discussing public policy, which is a recognized part of political science. Nonetheless, my university received an avalanche of criticism, including demands from prominent politicians that I be fired.

In one sense, the University of Calgary upheld my academic freedom. As I sat in my university office and wrote these words in spring 2013, I was still employed without any loss of salary or benefits. I had not been deprived of access to the library or computer system or prevented from working with graduate students. True, I retired at the end of June 2013, but that was my own decision, communicated to the university two months before the Incident. I am sixty-nine years old and have been teaching at the University of Calgary for forty-five years, so there's nothing odd about being ready for retirement. Academic freedom seems to have done what it is supposed to do – to prevent the university, no matter how great the political pressure, from inflicting economic damage upon a professor for something he has said related to his work of teaching, research, and community service.

But that description of the university's response to the Incident, while true, is not the whole truth. For a deeper understanding of the issues, we have to look carefully at the media release issued by President Elizabeth Cannon on February 28, 2013. Here is the final version (it was revised once during the course of the day):

> Comments made by Tom Flanagan in Lethbridge yesterday absolutely do not represent the views of the University of Calgary. In the university's view, child pornography is not a victimless crime. All aspects of this horrific crime involve the exploitation of children. Viewing pictures serves to create more demand for these terrible images, which leads to further exploitation of defenseless children.
>
> Tom Flanagan has been on a research and scholarship leave from the University of Calgary since January of 2013.

Tom Flanagan will remain on leave and will retire from the university on June 30, 2013. Flanagan had submitted his letter of retirement on Jan. 3, 2013.

Several things are seriously wrong with this statement. First, its claim to represent "the views of the University of Calgary" about child pornography should make every professor shudder. A university that respects academic freedom should not claim to take an institutional position on matters that are properly the subject of inquiry. The university hires and provides a working environment for academics who take positions as a result of their research and reflection. That's the point of the whole system, to guarantee that positions are based on study and reason. A university could only take a collective position, whether it's on child pornography or the theory of relativity, by some political process, either by counting votes or by the personal decision of those charged with running the institution. Neither decision-making process is adequate to the ambitions of science and scholarship, where the correct position is the one that can survive the clash of ideas, not the one that can win votes or curry favour with powerful administrators.

Of course, a university has to take positions in the course of running its own affairs as an organization. At various times, it may have to decide whether to sponsor military research as part of a country's war effort or law-enforcement research as part of a war on drugs. Today, unless a Canadian university wants to lose all federal research money, it has to endorse policies of employment equity for women, visible minorities,

Aboriginal peoples, and people with disabilities. Taking organizational positions on these, and a thousand other issues, is unavoidable in a world where universities are large enterprises with tens of thousands of students, thousands of employees, and dozens of buildings to administer. But that's different from claiming to have a collective position on the intellectual merits of an issue. Even if a university commits itself to support the war effort, or the war on drugs, or employment equity for purportedly disadvantaged groups, academic freedom means that any professor or student should be able to say, without reprisals from the institution, that the commitment is wrong-headed because the policy is misconceived.

President Cannon's statement must have been drafted in haste by public relations specialists with no time to consult genuine experts. Not surprisingly, therefore, it is a farrago of conventional wisdom – that child pornography is "not a victimless crime," that "all aspects of it involve the exploitation of children," and that "viewing pictures serves to create more demand for these terrible images." But in fact all of these statements are subject to debate in the scientific and legal literature about child pornography (more on this in the next chapter). They may not be wholly false, but neither are they entirely true. A presidential media release is not the right place to deal with such complexities.

Not only did the release wrongly state that the University of Calgary has a collective view on child pornography, but it implied that I have a different view ("Comments made by Tom Flanagan yesterday in Lethbridge absolutely do not represent . . ."). Since the main point of the release is moral denunciation of child pornography, the strong implication is that I must approve or at least be tolerant of child pornography. In fact, nothing could be more false. But in the world of public policy, the question ought to be not who can make the loudest, noisiest condemnation of evil, but what, if anything, can be done about it that would make a real difference without creating a new class of victims. If university administrators had taken the trouble to talk to me before rushing into the media with their release, they could easily have found out what my views are, rather than basing them on a YouTube video with a false tagline.

That's all by way of deconstructing the first paragraph. Sadly, it gets worse after that. What possible reason was there to say, "Tom Flanagan has been on a research and scholarship leave from the University of Calgary since January of 2013"? Whether I was or was not on sabbatical had nothing to do with what I reportedly said. The message is subliminal: Flanagan is not a threat to your children at the university because he's not actually teaching here now. The implication is strengthened by the further statement that I "will remain on leave and will retire from the university on June 30, 2013." What did my retirement have to do with it? Again, subliminal messaging: you don't have to worry about Flanagan corrupting the youth of Calgary because he's going away forever.

Even worse, the final sentence of the release ("Flanagan had submitted his letter of retirement on Jan. 3, 2013") was not included in the first version of the release, which went out shortly after noon on February 28. Read without the final sentence, the release seems to suggest that I had been pushed into retirement because of what I had said in Lethbridge. Head-lines to that effect echoed around the country. The final sentence was only added several hours later, after I had a con-versation with Richard Sigurdson, the dean of arts.

The joint effect of all the innuendos – that I was tolerant of child pornography, that I was not fit to teach, and that I was being pushed into retirement – was very injurious to my reputa-tion. Damage to one's reputation is a form of economic reprisal – exactly the sort of thing that academic freedom is supposed to prevent. In my case, there was direct and immediate financial loss, including the cancellation of my CBC and my Wildrose Party contracts and several paid speaking invitations. The Uni-versity of Calgary did not cause these economic repercussions all by itself, but President Cannon's media release was a contrib-uting factor. It's one thing to be denounced by politicians but an even worse indictment of your competence to be trashed by your employer of forty-five years.

Several lawyers told me that President Cannon's release was arguably defamatory, but I had no desire to sue the institu-tion where I have happily worked for so many years. Rather, I chose to grieve through our faculty association (TUCFA), and that led to a happy ending. After behind-the-scenes discussions that did not involve me personally, President Cannon issued the following letter of regret to a TUCFA officer:

> I am in receipt of a notice that the Faculty Association has filed a Step One grievance . . . relating to the statement I used on February 28, 2013 in regards to Dr. Tom Flanagan.

I understand that Dr. Flanagan has expressed concerns to the Faculty Association that the confidentiality of his employment information was breached and that the statement made misconstrued the circumstances and reasons for his research and scholarship leave, as well as his retirement.

Upon review, I realize that it was unnecessary to include the employment information in the statement. Please extend my regrets to Dr. Flanagan.

It was a rather minimalist statement, but I could live with it. People make mistakes (God knows I've made more than enough for one lifetime). The president admitted her mistake, and I sent her a note of appreciation for her willingness to do so. I'm not going to let one discordant episode ruin my memories of the University of Calgary, which has treated me exceptionally well for forty-five years. I look forward to continuing to teach one course a year at the University of Calgary's School of Public Policy. Director Jack Mintz, other colleagues at the school, and their students were unanimous in their desire to have me continue, and they told the university so. I will always be grateful for that.

Sheila Miller, TUCFA executive director, was of great help, but I got less support elsewhere. I called Jim Turk, CAUT executive director, to say that in my opinion the university's media release had violated my academic freedom. He assured me that CAUT was already on the case and was going to do something about it. Here is the letter that CAUT sent to President Cannon on March 11:

The Canadian Association of University Teachers has been following the media storm caused by Dr. Tom Flanagan's remarks recorded surreptitiously at an event at the University of Lethbridge on February 28 of this year. At its March 2013 meeting CAUT's Academic Freedom and Tenure Committee discussed his remarks and the fallout from them.

While we note that the senior administration has taken no formal action against Dr. Flanagan as a result of those comments, thereby avoiding violation of his academic freedom, we are concerned that, in your public statements about Dr. Flanagan, you claimed to be speaking for the entire university.

Though you are perfectly entitled to state your own views, you have neither the right nor the authority to appropriate the voices and opinions of the entire University of Calgary academic community. Your action sets a dangerous example, putting damage control ahead of expressive rights and responsibilities. There is a slippery slope here that leads only too readily to the silencing and purging of scholars in the name of orthodoxy or in response to public outcry.

This was a good letter inasmuch as it vigorously criticized President Cannon's pretence of speaking for the entire university, calling that "a dangerous example, putting damage control ahead of expressive rights and responsibilities." Unfortunately, however, CAUT did not deal with the university's assault on my reputation and the economic damage caused by that assault. It seemed to assume that academic freedom was only

a matter of not being fired ("we note that the senior administration has taken no formal action against Dr. Flanagan as a
result of those comments, thereby avoiding violation of his
academic freedom"), and that other kinds of economic reprisals were not relevant. President Cannon was later able to use
these words to defend her action in General Faculties Council,
saying that even CAUT recognized that the university had not
violated my academic freedom.

Unfortunately, CAUT did not consult further with me or
with Sheila Miller before composing this letter, thus missing a
chance to explore a dimension of academic freedom that will
probably become more relevant as time goes on. Because of
financial pressures, universities are hiring fewer tenured staff
and relying more on part-time and temporary appointments.
Such staff members, who by definition lack the protection of
tenure, are more easily subjected to other forms of economic
pressure regarding renewal of their temporary appointments,
permission to teach summer school, assignment to teach in
favoured courses, and so on. Economic reprisal other than
dismissal is highly relevant to the brave new world that universities are entering, so it is a pity that CAUT missed a
chance to deal with it.

The Society for Academic Freedom and Scholarship
(SAFS) had sent an even stronger letter to the University of
Calgary on March 8:

> We write to express our concern with your remarks that you
> posted on the university's website, Feb. 28. . . . These

remarks undermine academic freedom on your campus and send a discouraging message to the university community that the academic right to speak candidly about controversial topics may run afoul of the university's views on a range of social issues. In our experience, university presidents rightly do not claim that their universities hold views on controversial issues. For example, Martha Piper, former president of the University of British Columbia, faced with a controversial statement by a UBC faculty member, said in a speech at the Liu Centre at UBC on October 9, 2001:

> In all this it must be emphasized that the University as an institution holds no "views." I have often been asked what is the "University's" view on a variety of controversial issues – abortion, for example, or Aboriginal land claims, or provincial tax policy. What needs to be understood is that there is no such thing as a "University" view on such issues; rather, the University is a community of scholars with a wide range of views and opinions. Accordingly, the view of one scholar cannot and does not represent the view of the University.

It is clear to us that this statement is the correct position for a university president to take when confronted with controversial statements made by a member of faculty.

We would also note that your comments declaring that U of C, as an institution, has an opinion on child pornography, implies that Professor Flanagan is in opposition to the university's position, and leaves the clear impression that he supports child pornography and the exploitation of children.

It is obvious that Professor Flanagan does not support child pornography, because, as he wrote in his *National Post* op-ed (March 4), he endorses jail sentences for the production and delivery of child pornography. He further explained that what he was trying to do at the Lethbridge talk was raise the question of whether the best way to deal with consumers of child pornography was to incarcerate them rather than provide them with counseling.

In short, President Cannon, you censured one of your professors for expressing an opinion. Such an act is contrary to the purpose of the university. Again, quoting Martha Piper in the same speech we referred to earlier:

> The institution's role is to provide a forum for the free exchange of ideas, so that through critical analysis and discussion we may move closer to an understanding of our problems, and – we hope – to the discovery of solutions.
>
> Academic freedom simply refers to the protection of professors and their institutions from political interference. It asserts that in the university, unconventional ideas and controversial opinions deserve special protection.

We ask that you post on your university's website a reaffirmation of your and U of C's commitment to academic freedom. In addition, posting an apology to Professor Flanagan for violating his academic freedom would repair some of the damage done by your previously posted comments.

The SAFS letter was clearer than the CAUT letter on the crucial point that the university had violated academic freedom by imputing to me a position that I did not express and do not hold. It was great to get the moral support, but I doubt there was any practical impact. SAFS is a small organization (full disclosure: I am on the board of directors but removed myself from anything dealing with my case), with a mailing list of a few hundred. It is in no way comparable to CAUT, which, through affiliation with all the faculty unions in the country, has tens of thousands of members. In fact, President Cannon did not reply to either the CAUT letter or the SAFS letter. In that respect, she continued the unenviable reputation that the University of Calgary has established in recent years of ignoring critics of its actions in academic freedom cases (trying to suppress poster displays by pro-life students, threatening reprisals against students who criticized an instructor), both of which ended up in court.

Other threats to academic freedom in my case came from the demands of politicians that I be fired. Manitoba MP Joy Smith wrote in an op-ed distributed across the country: "I congratulate the Wildrose Party for firing him as their campaign manager; the CBC for firing him as their guest commentator on Power and Politics and the Manning Centre for removing him as a speaker at the upcoming Manning Conference."

Smith did not specifically call upon the University of Calgary to fire me, and maybe no one took her too seriously because she is a permanent ornament on the Conservative backbench.

Two other interventions, however, were more ominous. Alberta MLA Thomas Lukaszuk said archly that the provincial government would not pressure the university to fire me, but he was confident that the university's board of governors would "make the right decision. If anyone in my office was to make a comment of this sort, by now they would be lining up in the unemployment line." Lukaszuk is not just a run-of-the-mill backbencher. He is deputy premier of Alberta and minister of advanced education and training. He is not only second-in-command to Premier Alison Redford but also the minister directly responsible for Alberta's universities and colleges. It is disturbing that someone in his position would not understand the difference between political staff in his own office and tenured employees in a university. It is even more alarming that Premier Redford, who is a lawyer (indeed, she is often described as an international human rights lawyer), would tolerate this key minister trying to pressure the University of Calgary in such a way.

The most explicit demand to fire me came from British Columbia MP James Moore: "The demand for child pornography fuels the supply for child pornography. Any defence is unacceptable and disgusting. The CBC did the right thing by firing Tom Flanagan. I think the University of Calgary should take similar steps." Like Lukaszuk, Moore is not a powerless backbencher. At the time, he was the minister of Canadian heritage, through whom the CBC reports to Parliament. It was highly improper for him to be commenting in public on CBC personnel decisions, because the CBC is supposed to be an independent agency run by its executive staff under the control of its appointed board of governors. In his portfolio, Moore was also responsible for many cultural and scholarly programs that are important to Canadian universities. He didn't have direct control over universities in the way that Thomas Lukaszuk does, but he was certainly influential.

Lukaszuk and Moore did not pay any political price for their attempts to interfere with academic freedom. Lukaszuk remains deputy premier of Alberta and minister of advanced education and training. Moore was promoted in July 2013 from minister of Canadian heritage to minister of industry. He is widely praised in the media as a star performer for the Harper government and sometimes mentioned as a possible leadership candidate after Harper retires.

I am not aware of any pushback from the academic world against these blatant examples of political interference. No university presidents, faculty unions, or scholarly associations have spoken out to defend tenure against political threats. Experience has taught me the risks of antagonizing powerful politicians, but I think the long-term risks for academic freedom are even greater if university people do not defend their turf against interference, not just from political non-entities but from very high-ranking political figures.

Another threat to academic freedom came unexpectedly from the world of publishing. On March 4, 2013, I received the following email from Bruce Wallace, editor of *Policy Options* magazine:

> Tom. I am among those critical of your remarks in Leth-
> bridge. I do not challenge your right to speak freely on any
> topic. I take issue, in the strongest terms, with your state-
> ment that viewing child pornography does not cause harm
> to children. That statement reflects values that are deeply at
> odds with my own. As a result, I will not publish your work
> in the magazine I edit.

To understand what was going on here, you have to know the backstory.

*Policy Options* is a glossy monthly magazine published by the Institute for Research on Public Policy (IRPP) in Montreal. It is not a refereed journal in the academic sense, but it is widely distributed in government offices, and some journalists follow it as well. I have contributed to it half a dozen times in the past. In November 2012, I took part in an Elections Canada consultation in Montreal hosted by the IRPP. While I was there, that organization's new president, Graham Fox, asked if I would contribute another article to *Policy Options*. I said yes and suggested something on the Calgary Centre by-election that was scheduled to take place in a couple of weeks. The contest was drawing quite a bit of attention, so I thought *Policy Options* readers, at least the political junkies among them, might be interested in the clash of campaign strategies taking place beneath the surface. I hired a graduate student to help me with the data analysis, and we were just about ready to send the article to *Policy Options* when I got the email from Bruce Wallace, whom I have never met in person because he is a newly appointed editor.

In itself, Wallace's sudden refusal to publish my work was only a minor irritation. *Policy Options* doesn't pay anything to authors, and I will use the by-election article as an appendix to my next book on political campaigning. Nor do I contest the editor's legal right to refuse publication. American journalist A. J. Liebling famously wrote, "Freedom of the press is guaranteed only to those who own one," and the IRPP owns *Policy Options*. Q.E.D. I had no contract with *Policy Options*, and the editor can do what he wants. He is not bound by peer review, as he would be if *Policy Options* were a scholarly journal.

Nonetheless, I couldn't let this pass. A career in science and scholarship requires the opportunity to publish in academic journals and university presses but also in more popular outlets. It is an egregious threat to academic freedom for an editor to ban an author from his journal's pages simply because he does not like what he perceives to be the author's "values" on some unrelated subject. It is even worse in this case because the editor could have no real idea of what I think about child pornography, based on the distorted press coverage that prevailed during the Incident.

I forwarded my correspondence with Wallace to Jonathan Kay at the *National Post*, and he and Terence Corcoran took Wallace to task for shutting me out. Wallace replied in a long and angry post on the IRPP Facebook page. Farcically, he criticized the *National Post* columnists for not having taken the trouble to consult him before writing, when he hadn't taken the trouble to consult with me before deciding to reject my article.

I still have trouble understanding the logic of Wallace's position, as expressed in the final paragraph of his post:

> Mr. Flanagan can speak on any topic in any venue that will have him, a choice we at *Policy Options* retain as well. I share the position of some of his defenders that there is legitimate room to debate whether jailing people for viewing child pornography is the most appropriate or effective response. But it was Mr. Flanagan's cavalier declaration that this is an activity without victims that led to our decision to not publish his work, based on an irreconcilable conflict with the values of our magazine.

I never made a declaration that child pornography is an activity without victims. In fact, I never made a declaration at all; I just asked a question about the extent to which imprisonment is necessary for people who have done nothing except look at child pornography. I was obviously driving toward John Stuart Mill's famous distinction between direct and indirect harm, which Wallace could easily have discovered by phoning or emailing me before making his decision. And what do values have to do with it? Like most people, I think looking at child pornography is wrong, morally degrading, and often leads to worse things. But the question of public policy is, what should the state do about it? That's a matter of practical judgment, not an ethical issue of expressing values.

With Wallace and the IRPP digging in, I decided to widen the struggle a bit. I sent letters to the presidents of two academic organizations to which I belong, the Canadian Political Science Association (CPSA) and the Royal Society of Canada, suggesting that being banned from the pages of a journal over perceived values was an affront to academic freedom. The Royal Society decided that it wasn't their problem, which I think is a short-sighted attitude. An organization that boasts that its members are the leading scientists and scholars in Canada ought to be concerned when one of those members is prevented from publishing on such flimsy grounds. The Canadian Political Science Association took the matter a little more seriously, electing to try quiet diplomacy. The CPSA president called Wallace for a discussion, then reported back to me that perhaps my banishment was not permanent. I doubt that I'll bother writing for *Policy Options* again, but I appreciate that the CPSA at least tried to do something.

Overall, our academic organizations didn't earn a very high grade for protecting academic freedom, showing the power of moral panic to affect the thinking of even the most intelligent and rational of people. The University of Calgary put out press releases that egregiously damaged my reputation. CAUT took a minimalist view of what academic freedom means. The Royal Society didn't want to get involved. No one in the academic world seems to have been bothered by the spectacle of blowhard politicians demanding that the

university fire an academic staff member in defiance of contract law and even the most minimal understanding of
academic freedom. If this is how the Canadian academic world
reacts to a minor threat to academic freedom, what will
happen when something really serious comes along? Will academic organizations be roused to action, or will they be too
afraid to push back against politicians exploiting ill-informed
public opinion? I wish I could be optimistic.

## Teaching

Academic freedom is not just for loud-mouthed professors
seeking to make headlines; it is equally important to students
for the quality of their university education. This comes across
more strongly in the original German phrase *Lehrfreiheit und
Lernfreiheit* ("freedom to teach and freedom to learn") than in
the English phrase *academic freedom*. Of course, some of the
details are different. In the nineteenth-century German model,
*Lehrfreiheit* meant the freedom of professors not only to say
what they wanted but to offer whatever course of lectures
they wanted; and *Lernfreiheit* meant not only the right of students to attend, or not attend, whatever lectures they wished
but even to move from one university to another. Mass education on the North American model offers a different balance
of rights and opportunities to staff and students, but it is still
true that academic freedom is just as important to students'
learning as it is to professors' research and public service.

I've read some of the literature on university teaching, but I'm going to discuss it based primarily on my own experience. I've taught primarily at the University of Calgary but also as a visiting professor at the University of Alberta, McGill, and the Free University of Berlin. I've taught at every level, from first-year introductory courses to Ph.D. supervision, but the first year has always been my bread and butter. Together with colleagues, I co authored an introductory text for Canadian students, entitled *Introduction to Government and Politics: A Conceptual Approach.* Having appeared first in 1982, it's now in its ninth edition and is still widely used in Canadian universities and colleges.

I've also taught in almost every format, from large lectures with hundreds of students to personal guided readings, and everything in between. I've taught meditations on the Great Books as well as statistical methodology and survey research. I've drawn on simple mathematics to create a course in game theory for Canadians, and I've drawn on biology and anthropology for a course on the evolutionary interpretation of human political behaviour. (My favourite class was always the one where I had to explain why the male human penis was so much thicker, and the testicles so much smaller, than those of the male chimpanzee, and what that meant for differences in social structure and political behaviour.) At various times, I've also trespassed on the fields of literature, religious studies, history, and philosophy because politics extends its tentacles everywhere.

I don't claim to be a master teacher. I've never written anything on how to teach. I've never won a national or even university-wide prize for the quality of my teaching, though I did garner a couple of small awards from political science students in our own department. But I think I gave some of my students what they needed (maybe not what they wanted, at least at first). My teaching evaluations, for what they're worth, have always been above average – and not just in Garrison Keeler's sense of Lake Wobegon, where "all the children are above average." Some students have made a point of telling me how much the course meant to them, and some have stayed in touch. Not all, of course. I'm sure there were others who were glad never to have to see me again.

But that's precisely the point I want to make. There's no one way to be a good teacher, any more than there is a single way to be a jazz musician or a comedian or a baseball player. Like these other pursuits, teaching is a performance, initiated with planning but consummated with improvisation. And improvisation requires freedom.

Think about what's involved in university teaching. First of all, you're trying to communicate large amounts of new information to students. Yes, information is still vital, even in the age of the Internet. An educated person still needs a well-stocked mind in order to know what to search for and how to evaluate what you find. Conveying information means selecting the right readings and designing a sequence of classroom lectures and discussions to reinforce those readings. Lots of time might be spent giving carefully organized, informative lectures, using PowerPoint or whatever the next big thing may be. But even for the purpose of communicating information, there has to be more to it than straight lecturing. University class periods typically last fifty, seventy-five, or one hundred and fifty minutes. Even the shortest of these, the standard fifty-minute Monday-Wednesday-Friday class, is longer than the average person's attention span, which is more like thirty minutes, even on a good day. If you just get up and deliver straight information, you will lose most of your audience halfway through.

Even the most factual lecture, therefore, has to be paced and broken up in various ways just to fulfill the mandate of delivering information. Experienced teachers use jokes, quips, sidebar comments, anecdotes, and questions to keep the audience from tuning out. Here's a joke I've often used in introducing the dry-as-dust topic of Canadian federalism:

> At an international boarding school, the teacher assigns an essay on elephants. The French student hands in an essay entitled "The Love Life of the Elephant." The German student writes "Elephants: A Short Introduction in Four Volumes." The American boy describes "How to Build Bigger and Better Elephants." What does the Canadian student hand in? "Elephants: A Federal or Provincial Responsibility?"

It's mildly funny, and it illustrates better than ten minutes of lecture time how pervasive federalism is in Canadian politics. It has also become slightly edgy because national stereotypes appear in the story, but you can still get away with it because you're making fun of North Americans and Western Europeans.

Sometimes I play musical selections in class for a similar purpose. When explaining the concept of charisma, I have sometimes played Andrew Lloyd Webber's song from *Evita,* "Don't Cry for Me, Argentina" because it illustrates the inter-weaving of the personal and the political that gives force to charismatic leadership. Once, when teaching a graduate seminar on Friedrich Hayek, I played Reba McEntire's wonder-ful song "One Promise Too Late." In the middle of his life, Hayek left his wife for a woman he had loved as a young man. Reba's words don't exactly fit Hayek's situation (he broke his promise, whereas she kept hers, at least in the song), but they're close enough to hammer home the point I wanted to make, that even the greatest philosophers face all the prob-lems of ordinary people, and that their dilemmas can influence what they write.

Or, when briefly mentioning Hayek's importance to a large introductory class in the midst of a sequence of serious slides, I'll put up a slide of Selma Hayek wearing a white low-cut dress and sitting in a swing and say, "Not the real Hayek." It gets stu-dents' attention back to the PowerPoint, that's for sure!

These few stories are meant to illustrate that, even at the most basic level of delivering information, teaching is a coop-erative enterprise between professor and students. As a teacher, you use all your resources – the way you dress, your physical gestures and facial expressions, your tone of voice – as well as your words – your jokes and quips, your stories, your quotations from other sources – to engage your students. You're not just talking to them. If that were all that's involved, it would be lot cheaper just to set up a big-screen monitor and address thousands of people simultaneously. But students need to be engaged with a living instructor. They should feel that they're part of a joint enterprise. Even laughing on cue is an action that makes them part of the team. If I could figure out how to do it in a lecture hall, I would have them up dancing because rhythmic motion accompanied by music is the most powerful means of engagement ever discovered.

With engagement comes risk. The instructor has to take chances to break through the engagement barrier. You tell a joke and it might fall flat. Students might not appreciate your stories of what it was like to study in Europe in the 1960s. They might not see the point of your references to popular culture because they don't watch the same shows or listen to the same music as you. They might realize you're old (okay, they already know that). And students have to run risks too. They have to take the greatest chance of all – opening their minds and hearts to someone they barely know, trusting him to lead them toward treasures of knowledge and understanding that they can only dimly imagine.

A professor is not a parent, but there is something parental about the relationship between student and teacher. After half a century, I can still get misty-eyed thinking about the teachers who did so much for me. Father John Flattery got me to the point where I could painfully decode Cicero and Vergil with the help of a Latin dictionary, and I felt I had tapped into the wisdom of the ages. Seymour Gross, my first-year English teacher at Notre Dame, taught me how to read a work of literature. He also broke down my adolescent writing style and built it up again to a more adult standard. Gerhart Niemeyer introduced me to scholarship in the grand German mode. Allan Kornberg, the "Kosher Krusher," showed me the beauty of numbers in the substructure of human society and politics. I'm sure there were many other professors just as good or even better, but these men were *my* teachers, and the debt I owe them is beyond measure and can be redeemed only by "paying it forward," as the saying goes.

There are not a lot of good things I can say about the Incident, but one positive feature is that former students got in touch to offer their support. After Michael Enright discussed the Incident on the CBC Radio show *Sunday Edition*, one former student wrote in response:

> I had Tom Flanagan as a professor at the University of Calgary in the early 70's. I can just hear him create the argument that he formulated. He challenged my thoughts and issues of concern, always principled and always a demanding belief in the challenge of debate. . . .
>
> Tom Flanagan and I part ways on how to govern, but we are in complete agreement on the right to debate and discuss the issues of the day.
>
> It is sad in our society that we must now be "correct" in our thinking. This has hollow resonance back to the dark days of the cold war and the demand for conformation to the group think.

This kind of response is what I value above all in students – coming to their own conclusions, even (or especially) when they're different from my own. As the philosopher Nietzsche said, "He who always remains a student badly repays his teacher."

Another and more recent student also comes to mind. He took my course on political campaigning, and it was great to have him in the class because, as a committed Liberal (not that common in Alberta), he was often at odds with others in the class. A year later he came back to tell me he had used what he learned from about campaigning to get himself elected to the Students Legislative Council. Now he's on the university's Board of Governors (have I created a Liberal monster?). He still drops by occasionally to talk about the problems of the Alberta Liberals, which are enormous. He asks me what his party can do to improve, and I say, "Well, if I were the Liberal leader, here's what I'd consider doing." That's what makes the university such a wonderful place, that a former Conservative/Wildrose campaign manager can get together with a Liberal former student for a friendly conversation about how the Liberals could do better.

Of course, not all former students keep in touch and drop by for friendly chats. I'm sure that many over the years have left my classes hoping never to see me again. They may have thought that I was boring, or told too many stories, or graded too hard. Their perceptions may have been quite accurate – for them. There is no single model of good teaching; nothing works with all students.

That's why academic freedom is so important. Professors have to have room to discover what works well for them, in their discipline, with their personality, with their particular bundle of strengths and weaknesses. Typical undergraduate students at a large university will be exposed to perhaps three dozen instructors in the course of getting a bachelor's degree. Out of those three dozen, they will probably find a small handful that seemed especially memorable and another handful that seemed like a complete waste of time or worse. But the variety gives all students a chance to find at least a few inspirational professors whose memory can be cherished for a lifetime. If that doesn't happen, the student has been cheated.

When we get beyond the first level of teaching, the distribution of information, the relationship between teacher and student becomes even more intense. Professors worthy of their hire face at least three challenges beyond communicating information. First, you have to awaken students' interest in topics of whose importance they have no idea and of which they probably have never even heard. Machiavelli's *Prince*. Regression equations. Supreme Court decisions. It's not so simple to make these topics compete for space in students' mind with their usual amusements of sex, drugs, and rock 'n' roll.

Then you want them to ask important questions about such topics. Did Machiavelli teach that the ends justify the means? Do they? Does political raison d'état override normal morality? What is the difference between correlation and causation? How can we use statistical controls to narrow down potential relationships between variables? How aggressive should the Supreme Court be in overturning legislation passed by Parliament? By provincial legislatures?

Finally, you want to expand their horizons for future study. You want them to learn that reading old books like the *Prince* is a particularly good pathway to wisdom. Precisely because the book is so old, its context is totally different from the students' own lives, thus forcing them to grapple with essential questions without the props of familiar experience, customs, and institutions. You want them to know that regression is a basic tool in all the empirical sciences, both natural and social, and that the statistical reasoning they use in figuring out who votes for whom is fundamentally the same as the thought process involved in testing the efficacy of new medicines. And you want them to see that law is a noble intellectual enterprise, the undergirding of all civilization, not just the ticket to a lucrative career.

These higher-order goals of university teaching require enhanced mental activity by students. Taking notes about how important the *Prince* is won't give them a love of classic works of political philosophy. They have to ask and answer questions. Here's how you might go about it as an instructor. You know that Machiavelli was imprisoned and tortured for getting on the wrong side in Florentine politics. Show the students an Internet picture of the *strappado* and talk briefly about broken arms and dislocated shoulders. Ask them what the *Prince* says about the treatment of individuals. Does Machiavelli assume that rulers can and should treat other people the same way he was treated? If so, is that political realism or a form of evil that we hope we've outgrown, apart from some occasional waterboarding?

Another example: When I teach courses covering social assistance and the welfare state, I usually begin by asking, "Why don't we just leave the indigent to starve on the streets?" That's not a statement, it's a question, to which there are lots of good answers. But the answers are quite varied and lead to very different policies. Is social assistance a right that the poor have under the prevailing conception of social justice? Is it, as Marxists often argue, a strategy of the ruling class to forestall social revolution? Or, as argued by American scholar Marvin Olasky, is social assistance something that government shouldn't offer at all because families, churches, synagogues, and other private organizations will do it more effectively? Asking the original question in such a seemingly callous manner is a kind of intellectual electroshock. It forces students to forget what they've always taken for granted and go back to first principles to develop a justifiable policy. Not all will agree on what the principles and policy should be, but the disagreement is a necessary part of the process.

Classes often work better if they contain some Marxists, feminists, fundamentalist Christians, or other outlying opinion groups, as long as they are willing to join in the game of asking and answering. But it can only work as long as everyone agrees that it is a game played for mutual benefit, not an opportunity to take down political opponents. Participants, both students and faculty, have to be free to explore radical and even offensive proposals. Is torture sometimes justified? Would the poor be better off without any state help? Should Canada be dissolved so that la nation Québécoise can assume its sovereignty? I personally would answer no to all of these questions, but I would be delighted to discuss any of them with a group of students; and I might assume a position that I don't actually hold for the purpose of driving the discussion forward. Discussions of this type are essential if students are to graduate from being passive recipients of information to active holders of knowledge, with maybe even a soupçon of creativity added to the mix.

Seen in this context, the phrase *taste in pictures* that I used at the University of Manitoba in 2009 was a typical classroom provocation, used to get students to realize that inflicting prison terms for viewing child pornography is a deliberate policy choice, is far from universal around the world, and is something to be examined rather than taken for granted. I wasn't teaching a scheduled class, but I was certainly in a teaching situation, having been invited by University of Manitoba professors to address a student audience in a university classroom in the middle of the day. That's what happens when you take teaching seriously: you may say things that sound callous, offensive, or even unhinged if taken out of context but that have a definite purpose within the process of higher education.

None of this can happen without academic freedom involving both *Lehrfreiheit und Lernfreiheit*. Both teacher and students have to be free to ask unconventional, even outrageous questions in the course of getting to the heart of the matter. You can't do this if you feel that someone is always watching you, ready to report you to the authorities if you challenge some canon of prevailing orthodoxy. The university classroom is often a venue for political discussion, but it also must be protected from politics in the sense of coalition-building.

A typical political meeting is the antithesis of a classroom discussion. Armed with prepared talking points, speakers come to deliver a disciplined message. They have been taught bridging techniques to escape from difficult questions ("that's not the question, this is the real question. . . ."). If it's an event staged by a single political party, the speaker is already talking to the converted, trying to reinforce their enthusiasm, not get them to probe their beliefs for contradictions. If the event is a debate among representatives of different parties, all the factions will have tried to stack the room with their own partisans. They don't come to learn something new but to make their opponents look bad. The goal is to generate something for the news that will win votes. It's the stuff of politics, but nothing could be more deadly to what is supposed to happen in a university classroom.

To return to my own Incident, I wasn't teaching a class at the University of Lethbridge, but I saw it as a class-like setting whose purpose was the discussion of issues, not the making of political points. Setting me up with a question irrelevant to the main topic, recording the interchange, and posting it on YouTube with a misleading tagline were political techniques designed to discredit me as a political opponent rather than engage in a rational discussion. Indeed, the crowd shouted me down as soon as I tried to answer the question that had been asked about child pornography – an infallible sign that politics is at play. Shouting people down never occurs in well-functioning university classrooms, whereas it is commonplace in political meetings. So I got trapped in the Incident by acting professorially rather than politically.

What happened to me in a class-like setting could, however, happen to any professor at any time in an actual classroom. Students could have their cellphones turned on and you wouldn't know it. Indeed, in large classes a student wouldn't even have to be enrolled in the course. If two hundred or even one hundred students are taking your class, you won't recognize someone new who shows up for the first time midway through the course in order to record you in a gaffe. Nor will you recognize the accomplice who asks a question designed to get you to say something provocative.

Of course, it won't happen all the time, or even very frequently. A lot of university subject matter doesn't lend itself to controversy, and many professors are just not very controversial. But I can foresee two obvious types of targets. One would be professors who have become prominent in politics or public affairs. If you're prominent, you almost surely have enemies. The other type of target would consist of professors who, while not individually prominent, work in incendiary fields, such as human sexuality. You can't teach in that area without addressing gay rights, infanticide, abortion, pornography, and a host of other issues fraught with controversy.

If I were not retiring from teaching, would I retreat from what I've always done in the classroom? I don't know. But I do know that some colleagues from across the country have emailed me saying they've seen what happened to me and are resolved to be more cautious in the classroom in the future. If that happens, students will be the losers. Today's professors have already had the benefit of open discourse in their past education. Students thirsting for the excitement of intellectual discovery will suffer the most if academic freedom is curtailed in the classroom.

## CHAPTER 7

# CHILD PORNOGRAPHY

## Defining Child Pornography

CHILD PORNOGRAPHY WAS NEVER PART OF MY
research portfolio, and I never expected to write anything about
it. The Incident, and this book I've written about it, grew out of
a single rhetorical question I had asked about child pornography when I was lecturing about something else. But having
become *persona non grata* by asking a question, I wanted to learn
more about the subject. I'm still no expert in the field and have
no plans to become one. But I've done enough reading and
reflection to see that Canadian law on child pornography raises
some serious questions – not surprising, considering how it was
shaped by moral panic and political opportunism.

Readers not familiar with section 163.1 of the Criminal
Code can read it below. Rather than attempt to summarize it, I
will plunge immediately into the difficulties that I see in it.

### Definition of child pornography

163.1 (1) In this section, "child pornography" means

(a) a photographic, film, video or other visual representation, whether or not it was made by electronic or mechanical means,

i) that shows a person who is or is depicted as being under the age of eighteen years and is engaged in or is depicted as engaged in explicit sexual activity, or

(ii) the dominant characteristic of which is the depiction, for a sexual purpose, of a sexual organ or the anal region of a person under the age of eighteen years;

(b) any written material, visual representation or audio recording that advocates or counsels sexual activity with a person under the age of eighteen years that would be an offence under this Act;

(c) any written material whose dominant characteristic is the description, for a sexual purpose, of sexual activity with a person under the age of eighteen years that would be an offence under this Act; or

(d) any audio recording that has as its dominant characteristic the description, presentation or representation, for a sexual purpose, of sexual activity with a person under the age of eighteen years that would be an offence under this Act.

### Making child pornography

(2) Every person who makes, prints, publishes or possesses for the purpose of publication any child pornography is guilty of

(a) an indictable offence and liable to imprisonment for a term not exceeding ten years and to a minimum punishment of imprisonment for a term of one year; or

(b) an offence punishable on summary conviction and is liable to imprisonment for a term not exceeding two years less a day and to a minimum punishment of imprisonment for a term of six months.

### Distribution, etc. of child pornography

(3) Every person who transmits, makes available, distributes, sells, advertises, imports, exports or possesses for the purpose of transmission, making available, distribution, sale, advertising or exportation any child pornography is guilty of

(a) an indictable offence and liable to imprisonment for a term not exceeding ten years and to a minimum punishment of imprisonment for a term of one year; or

(b) an offence punishable on summary conviction and liable to imprisonment for a term not exceeding eighteen months and to a minimum punishment of imprisonment for a term of ninety days.

### Possession of child pornography

(4) Every person who possesses any child pornography is guilty of

(a) an indictable offence and is liable to imprisonment for a term of not more than five years and to a minimum punishment of imprisonment for a term of six months; or

(b) an offence punishable on summary conviction and is liable to imprisonment for a term of not more than 18 months and to a minimum punishment of imprisonment for a term of 90 days.

### Accessing child pornography

(4.1) Every person who accesses any child pornography is guilty of

(a) an indictable offence and is liable to imprisonment for a term of not more than five years and to a minimum punishment of imprisonment for a term of six months; or

(b) an offence punishable on summary conviction and is liable to imprisonment for a term of not more than 18 months and to a minimum punishment of imprisonment for a term of 90 days.

### Interpretation

(4.2) For the purposes of subsection (4.1), a person accesses child pornography who knowingly causes child pornography to be viewed by, or transmitted to, himself or herself.

### Aggravating factor

(4.3) If a person is convicted of an offence under this section, the court that imposes the sentence shall consider as an aggravating factor the fact that the person committed the offence with intent to make a profit.

### Defence

(5) It is not a defence to a charge under subsection (2) in respect of a visual representation that the accused believed that a person shown in the representation that is alleged to constitute child pornography was or was depicted as being eighteen years of age or more unless the accused took all reasonable steps to ascertain the age of that person and took all reasonable steps to ensure that, where the person was eighteen years of age or more, the representation did not depict that person as being under the age of eighteen years.

### Defence

(6) No person shall be convicted of an offence under this section if the act that is alleged to constitute the offence

(a) has a legitimate purpose related to the administration of justice or to science, medicine, education or art; and

(b) does not pose an undue risk of harm to persons under the age of eighteen years.

### Question of law

(7) For greater certainty, for the purposes of this section, it is a question of law whether any written material, visual representation or audio recording advocates or counsels sexual activity with a person under the age of eighteen years that would be an offence under this Act.

## The Problem of Age

The Criminal Code now defines child pornography as any explicit sexual depiction or representation of a person who is, or is pretending to be, less than eighteen years of age. Such a definition doesn't fit very well with human biology and history. The age of marriage and initiation of sexual activity has varied widely across time and place but has almost always included the teenaged years. The age of consent to marriage in most Canadian provinces is sixteen (some, but not all, also require parental consent for young people under eighteen). In Shakespeare's famous play, we are told that Juliet is thirteen. In a modern Canadian version of *Romeo and Juliet,* Romeo could easily become a child pornographer if he owned a smartphone.

From the time they reach puberty, human beings are capable of sexual intercourse leading to conception, and they become extremely interested in sex at that time. You don't have to be a researcher to know that; anyone who's ever been a teenager will verify it. The average age of first menstruation for girls in the Western world is now twelve to thirteen, and thirteen for first ejaculation in boys. Those ages have been falling because of better nutrition and medical care; the comparable figures in the nineteenth century were more like fifteen for girls and sixteen for boys. Thus our Criminal Code has moved in a direction opposite to biological change. While our children are maturing and becoming physically ready for sexual experiments at an earlier age, we have raised the age for depicting teenage sexuality to a new high.

Into this ever-widening legal gap, enter the Internet and modern recording technology. Virtually every teenager now owns a mobile phone that doubles as a digital camera, video recorder, and audio recorder. They can create images of themselves and others engaged in sexual activity, just as they can of anything else they do. With little effort, they can send these images by email or post them to social media platforms. They can send them to sexual partners in a spirit of romantic affection, or they can distribute them widely out of vindictive revenge. It might all be child pornography from the point of view of the Canadian Criminal Code.

As a father and grandfather, I'm not particularly happy that kids can now record and distribute their sexual experiments. I hope we can find ways to restrain their impulse to do silly things, but they're teenagers, and they'll make lots of mistakes on the road to adulthood. I don't think anything is gained by bringing in the Criminal Code to define teenagers recording their sexual experiments as the creation of child pornography. Do we want trials and prison terms on top of the sexual anxiety, heartbreak, and humiliation that teenagers experience as they grow up?

It's not hard to imagine a realistic scenario. Sixteen-year-old boy and girl fall for each other and into bed. Boy takes nude pictures of girl in provocative positions. Boy and girl fall out of love, and boy emails pictures to his buddies to prove what a stud he is. Girl finds out and is humiliated. Girl's parents complain to police, who charge boy with possessing, making, and distributing child pornography. Everyone's life is ruined.

Clearly the boy has done something wrong, but calling it child pornography doesn't capture his betrayal of the girl's trust.

After I drafted the above paragraph, the heart-rending story of Rehtaeh Parsons again made headlines in Canada. Nova Scotia teen Rehtaeh (Heather spelled backward) Parsons had a sexual encounter with four boys at a house party in 2011, when she was fifteen. Her family later claimed it was rape, but two sets of prosecutors declined to lay sexual assault charges, fearing they could not obtain a conviction because testimony of witnesses was inconsistent and a lot of drinking was involved. The boys circulated a graphic photographic image of the encounter, causing Rehtaeh to feel harassed and bullied, even though she changed schools. After eighteen months of this, she committed suicide. After much unfavourable commentary from politicians and the public, charges of making and distributing child pornography were laid against two of the boys.

Looking at this from a distance, it seems only just that the boys be charged with *something*. Even if the act did not amount to sexual assault, distributing the picture was an evil thing to do. Yet what they did was not child pornography in any ordinary sense, which we usually think of as the manipulation of children by adults, not teenagers acting stupidly or viciously toward each other. The boys may not go to jail; their status as juveniles means the mandatory minimum sentences for child pornography won't apply. But they may be labelled as sex offenders, with incalculable consequences for their future (and, of course, Rehtaeh now has no future). Well-crafted cyber-bullying legislation is probably the right remedy for situations such as this; but, like the prohibition of hate propaganda, such legislation will not be easy to draft without interfering with freedom of speech.

Another issue of age involves the sexual desire that some mature men feel toward teenaged girls. In the technical literature, *hebephilia* refers to strong sexual attraction toward pubescent girls, roughly eleven- to fourteen- years old, while *ephebophilia* refers to attraction to slightly older teenaged girls, say fifteen to seventeen years of age. (There are also gay versions of both conditions, but I'm trying to keep it simple here.) In the contemporary world, we have many reasons to disapprove of older men pursuing teenaged girls. We have become committed to the general idea of equality between the sexes, and a relationship between a teenaged girl and an older man is likely to put her in a position of severe disadvantage.

Even though we properly condemn such relationships in the modern world, they are not unnatural in a biological sense; indeed, the American Psychiatric Association has recently rejected hebephilia as a medical diagnosis. Throughout history, men have pursued teenaged girls, and a girl's parents were often happy to promise their teenaged daughter in marriage to a wealthy and powerful man. There is a well-developed literature in evolutionary psychology about the nearly universal preference, among both men and women, for relationships in which the man is the older partner. The preference arises because human females, uniquely among mammalian species, have a limited period of fertility, extending between menarche and menopause. The human male, who remains fertile throughout his life, is naturally drawn to younger women in the course of maximizing his own reproductive potential.

Against this backdrop, adult male sexual interest in teen-aged girls is properly seen as an extension of the normal male interest in younger females. The terms *hebephilia* and *ephebo-philia* have been invented in our own day because such relationships are problematic in the type of society that we have become. Nothing wrong there – all societies have to discourage natural urges that are disruptive in their own context.

So, no, I don't want an older man hanging around my teen-aged daughter. But it's misleading to lump attraction for sexually mature teenagers together with sexual attraction toward pre-pubescent children. The latter constitutes pedophilia in the true sense. It is not an extension of a normal sexual urge but a deformation, a non-reproductive disruption of normal sexuality. Of course, every case is unique in some ways, but many pedophiles seem unable to sustain a sexual relationship with another adult and thus gravitate toward children.

The difference was brought home to me by a phone call I received in early March while my name was in the news. The caller was a man awaiting trial on charges of making child pornography. He described himself as a guy who liked girls. He had started a new business of making adult videos for legal distribution, but he hadn't checked the credentials of the girls he had paid to act, and some had turned out to be under eighteen even though they said they were older. Ergo, child pornography, with a possible ten-year sentence if he is convicted. I'm not enthused about his line of work, and there probably do need to be enforceable rules to prevent people who make such videos from using underaged girls. But the end product doesn't seem to me to have much to do with what we usually think of as child pornography.

## Inclusiveness

Section 163.1 of the Criminal Code is comprehensive in including all possible representations of child sexual activity. It explicitly mentions film, video, and audio recordings, as well as written materials and *visual representations*, a term that includes drawings and paintings as well as photographs. Indeed, the depiction does not have to be of a child under eighteen; it can be of "a person who . . . is depicted as being under the age of eighteen years," wording that includes adult actors dressed and made up to look like teenagers. Think of the popular television series *Glee*. When the series was launched in 2009, all of the eight major roles in the high school glee club were played by professional actors over the age of eighteen. Some of them are now in their late twenties or early thirties, yet they continue to give credible performances of teenagers.

Such comprehensiveness may be reasonable if the goal to include all possible representations of child sexuality; but in going this far, the legislation contradicts one of the most powerful arguments in favour of taking a tough stand against child pornography. At least as far back as the 1984 Badgley report, it has been repeatedly stated in absolute terms that all child pornography is evil and should be criminalized because it victimizes the real children used to produce it. Yet the wording of section 163.1 criminalizes many depictions of childhood sexuality that can be works of pure imagination without involving any real children:

- Stories and novels such as those of the famous writer Vladimir Nabokov (not just *Lolita*; the man was obsessed with nymphets – a word he contributed to the English language – and wrote several novels about adult males who are sexually attracted to them).
- Cartoons and drawings, such as Japanese *manga*. Child pornography is not illegal in Japan, and the country's graphic artists produce a lot of material that is exported around the world.
- Drawings and paintings by artists such as the internationally known Canadian Eli Langer, who exhibited works on childhood sexuality in Toronto in 1993, coinciding in time with passage of the first version of section 163.1 of the Criminal Code. Langer's works were seized by police but were eventually exonerated in court because they were deemed to have "artistic merit." The "artistic merit" qualification was subsequently taken out of section 163.1, so it is an open question whether Langer's exhibition would be legal in Canada today.
- Photographs and videos using adult actors playing teenagers. Put a kilt and a blazer on a young woman, give her the right makeup and hairstyle, and she can look like a high school student.

- Synthetic human representations generated with computer graphics software, like "Sweetie," the ten-year-old Filipino girl who was really a computer-generated avatar. The organization Terre des Hommes Netherlands ran an elaborate sting operation in 2013, using Sweetie to entice a thousand men from all over the world to offer payment to see her undressed or performing sexual acts.

Maybe all these types of literary, artistic, and graphic representations of child sexuality should be criminalized; I haven't been able to make up my mind on that. But what is clear to me is that the inclusion of all these materials undermines the statement, made so frequently and dogmatically, that *all* child pornography harms the children who have been used to make it. That statement can only be true of pornography in which actual children were employed.

## Virtue and Vice

Let's do a little etymology together. I find that looking into the origin of words often gives further insight into their meaning.

The English word *virtue* is derived from the Latin *virtus,* which is an extension of *vir,* meaning "man" in the sense of a male human being. *Virtus* is generally translated into English as "virtue," but the connotations were quite different in the Republican period of Roman history; a better translation might be "manliness." The man of *virtus* was courageous and self-controlled, concerned above all with maintaining his honour through devotion to his family and the Roman Republic. The English word *vice* is derived from the Latin *vitium*, which means "weakness." Vices such as avarice, gluttony, or unbridled sexual desire were seen as character flaws that weakened courage and self-control and could interfere with devotion to family and the Republic.

In the course of two thousand years of philosophical reflection and linguistic change, *virtue* has taken on many new meanings, but the original sense of *vice* as weakness survives more or less intact. Today we still use the term *vice* to include character flaws and patterns of behaviour that show lack of self-control, such as drunkenness, drug addiction, gambling, and resorting to prostitutes. Hence the term *vice squad* to designate the arm of the police imposing sanctions on such behaviour.

Vices involve social behaviour, to be sure. If you drink alcohol or use drugs, you have to buy the substances. If you gamble, you have to have a house or bookie to bet against. If you want to buy sex, you have to find someone to sell it. These are all social transactions but also voluntary. Thus the drug dealer is not victimized by the drug addict, nor the bookie by the gambler. Indeed, we often tend to see the victimization in reverse, as if the purveyor of vice is harming the customer by taking advantage of his weakness.

The harm from vice falls primarily upon the person who is prone to it. For example, alcoholics or drug addicts may lose their job through inability to function, and compulsive gamblers may lose all their money. Of course, the harm also radiates outward to their families and others. Alcoholics kill people on the highway, as do drug addicts. So alcoholism is a great social evil, but the harm comes not from the consumption of alcohol itself but from the irresponsible behaviour that it induces. In this respect, vices are different from crimes against persons and property, in which the harm is part of the act itself.

It is difficult to see much consistency in what is regarded as vice in different places and times. The Puritans saw dancing and card playing as forms of vice, but today these are considered harmless amusements and are the focus of popular television shows. In the second half of the nineteenth century, male masturbation was widely regarded as a vice because the loss of vital essence was thought to weaken the constitution. The rise of male circumcision as a routine procedure performed on baby boys was due in large measure to the belief that it would discourage masturbation. Today male masturbation is often recommended as a health measure, and it is referred to with amusement in popular entertainment, such as the famous "Contest" episode on *Seinfeld* (though it would be considered pornographic to actually show the act, and the word was not even used in the episode). Cigarette smoking, after being the height of sophistication in the mid-twentieth century, is now definitely a vice. The only people who smoke in contemporary movies and TV shows are villains and the severely stressed. Gluttony seems to be making a comeback as a vice as society tries to cope with the prevalence of obesity.

It is also difficult to see much consistency in the way vices are treated when they are recognized. In the nineteenth century,

alcoholism, which was an enormous social problem, was combatted with the moral measures of the temperance movement,
temperance being the virtue of moderation in consumption of
alcohol. In the early twentieth century, the United States and
several Canadian provinces went beyond temperance to legal
prohibition. When that was deemed a failure, medical
approaches emerged and still dominate, though much so-called
medical treatment is actually moral, as in the Twelve Steps of
Alcoholics Anonymous. Marijuana and other drugs have been
combatted with legal measures, but a medical approach is now
starting to take hold in this field, except in Canada, where the
Conservative government is trying to stiffen law enforcement
measures. In the fifty years of my own adult lifetime, I have seen
homosexuality regarded first as a sin and a crime, then as a
mental illness, and now as a blameless lifestyle choice or perhaps
a genetically determined behaviour.

The only safe generalizations seem to be that (1) societies
always stigmatize some human inclinations as vices; (2) the
common element in the enumeration of vices is the absence of
self-control, but beyond that the list of vices can vary greatly;
and (3) societies try to combat vices with moral, medical, and
legal means, selected and combined in no discernible pattern.

How does child pornography fit into this tableau? It seems
like another form of vice, a weakness of character that
degrades viewers themselves, but there is more to it. Some
viewers might derive erotic pleasure simply from images of
children's beautiful bodies, but in most cases the pornographic
image or story represents a child engaged in sexual activity,

either with adults or other children. Thus the essence of child pornography is the contemplation of something immoral, which distinguishes it from other vices. When alcoholics take a drink, or stoners light up a joint, or gamblers place a bet, they're not contemplating harm to anyone else. Harm may come indirectly to others, but it is not part of the activity itself. But viewing child pornography generally means becoming sexually aroused by contemplating something that is intrinsically wrong (forcing sex on a child too young to give informed consent). Vices such as alcoholism, drug addiction, and gambling may cause harm to others as an unintended consequence of pursuing pleasure, but child pornography is the pursuit of pleasure through contemplating harm to others.

As a starting point, this seems like a good reason to make child pornography illegal. If the actions depicted are immoral, illegal, and directly harmful to defenceless children, should we not outlaw pictures and stories whose purpose is to give sexual pleasure in the contemplation of such activities? Common sense suggests that the more people are led to take pleasure in thinking about evil actions, the more likely they are to carry them out.

The argument is persuasive, and yet it opens up uncertain vistas. We would hardly have any imaginative literature without the depiction of immoral and criminal activities. Sometimes criminals emerge victorious or even glorified; no doubt some readers and viewers get excited by the depiction of evil even when that is not the purpose of the work. Section 163 of the Criminal Code defines obscenity as the "undue exploitation" of sex, or of sex together with any one of "crime, horror, cruelty and violence." The term *undue exploitation* is obviously subjective and elastic, and much of today's popular entertainment would have been considered undue exploitation two generations ago. But we can argue about those questions some other time. For now, I'm happy to stipulate that all child pornography should be subject to legal sanctions because it is inseparable from the promotion of evil.

## Crime and Punishment

Agreeing that the law should be mobilized against child pornography is, however, the beginning, not the end of the analysis. Asserting that child pornography is not a victimless crime, and therefore should be punished, doesn't settle what the punishment should be. In all areas of the law, we assign degrees of culpability, with corresponding levels of punishment. Murder in Canada can be first degree, second degree, or manslaughter, depending on the perpetrator's intention, and punishments vary accordingly. Similarly, the Criminal Code differentiates sexual assault, sexual assault with a weapon, and aggravated sexual assault, with increasing levels of punishment for each. We follow the same principle outside of criminal law too. You'll get a stiffer fine for speeding 100 kilometres an hour over the limit than if you were only going 20 kilometres an hour too fast.

How might this principle apply to child pornography? Consider two imaginary offenders, call them John and Joe. John abuses his ten-year-old stepdaughter, gets her to perform oral sex on him, makes a video recording of the act, and posts it online so other members of his pedophile chat group can enjoy the spectacle. Joe takes a trip to Japan, buys a *manga* comic that includes a cartoon drawing of a child performing oral sex, and brings it back to Canada in his suitcase so he can reread it in the future. Would anyone dispute that John's actions are far more reprehensible than Joe's? John has created child pornography in the process of abusing a real child, and then compounded the offence by sharing the recording with others. Joe, in contrast, has not had contact with an actual child; he has only looked at a pictorial work of the imagination. Almost everyone, including me, would consider Joe's action wrong, but how heavily should it be punished? Under section 163.1 of the Criminal Code, it is possession of child pornography and carries a minimum punishment of three months in prison, even if the Crown proceeds in the more lenient way of summary conviction, or six months if the Crown proceeds by way of indictment.

What wrongs did Joe commit when he purchased and read the *manga* comic? Three things, at least. First he debased himself by contemplating with enjoyment an act that should never be performed by anyone – the sexual abuse of a child. Second, by buying the comic he contributed to the market for works of child pornography, helping to keep alive a business whose purpose is to promote vice. Third, by meditating upon a crime, he may have made himself more likely to commit such a crime in the future, by translating thought into action.

The offence has some similarities to possession and consumption of a banned drug – self-debasement, contributing to keeping an industry alive, and perhaps making oneself more likely to commit other criminal acts. Yet there is no minimum mandatory prison term for possession of even the most dangerous drugs in Schedule I of the Narcotics Act, such as heroin and cocaine. In fact, the *maximum sentence* if the Crown proceeds by way of summary conviction for possession of Schedule I drugs is the same as the *minimum sentence* if the Crown proceeds by way of indictment for possession of child pornography – six months.

Canadian law generally shows some lenience for simple possession or analogous offences. There is no mandatory minimum sentence for possession of hard or soft drugs. Many countries and American states are moving in the direction of decriminalizing possession altogether, though there may still be civil penalties. Simple possession of obscene materials other than child pornography is not even a criminal offence, though manufacture and distribution are. Hate speech is a crime in Canada, but that is defined as advocacy of genocide or incitement to violence against an identified group. In other words, you have to do something public to be guilty of the crime. A judge can order the confiscation of materials deemed to advocate hatred, but possession in itself is not a crime. Selling sex – prostitution – has never been illegal in Canada, although public solicitation for prostitution and keeping a brothel are criminal offences.

Each of these offences is unique, and the fact that the law treats adult obscenity, drugs, prostitution, and hate speech in one way does not necessarily mean that it should treat child pornography the same way. Yet there does seem to be a general principle at work here: recognizing a lowest level of offence that is either not criminalized or, if criminalized, does not carry a mandatory prison sentence. In all cases, those lowest levels of offence can be characterized as largely private activities – consuming drugs, enjoying obscene publications, hating groups of people, or engaging in sexual relations for money. We want to discourage all these, but we do not bring the full weight of the law to bear on the lowest, most private levels of offence. We mobilize the Criminal Code more actively against the public manifestations of these vices, such as advocating, distributing, selling, and advertising.

Against this backdrop, Canada's treatment of possession of child pornography seems particularly harsh. No other vice merits a mandatory prison term on a first conviction for the lowest and most nearly private level of offence. And other severe penalties are involved beyond the prison term. A criminal charge guarantees publicity, and the stigma around child pornography is huge. Loss of employment would be almost guaranteed, even before having to go away for a term in jail. Afterwards, your name is put on a nationwide sex offender registry, as well as a provincial registry in Ontario. The names on the Canadian registry are held in confidence, but in Ontario names may be disclosed to the community if the police think it is necessary for public safety. The information on corresponding federal and state registries in the United States is generally public, which makes it hard for offenders to re-establish a normal life after release from prison. In a few cases, offenders have been harmed or even killed by vigilantes.

But surely, one might think, public security, especially the safety of children, comes first. Police have to be able to keep tabs on known sex offenders, and communities have a right to be informed if dangerous people are in their midst. I endorse the primacy of public safety, but applying the concept to child pornography is far from straightforward. There is little solid scientific evidence on how likely consumers of child pornography are to commit sexual assaults against children.

It is often reported that convicted pedophiles have used child pornography. That is hardly surprising; people tend to watch and read about activities that they're interested in. But even if *all* convicted pedophiles enjoyed child pornography, that wouldn't tell us how likely it is that a user of child pornography will go on to commit a sexual offence against children. To calculate that probability, we would have to know the denominator of the fraction, that is, how many users of child pornography there are; and that information is completely lacking. Viewing child pornography is illegal and highly stigmatized, so people do it in secrecy and are loath to admit it unless caught. To draw a parallel, probably everyone convicted of murder has seen violent movies, but that doesn't prove watching violent movies leads to murder because violent movies are ubiquitous and almost everyone has seen them.

Because the data we would like to have are simply unavailable, researchers have to pursue other strategies, such as the study of recidivism. Important work of this type has been done by forensic psychologist Michael Seto of the University of Toronto. In a study published in 2011, Seto and collaborators reported the results of following 541 offenders listed in the Ontario Sex Offender Registry. Of these, 228 had been convicted of child pornography offences only. Below are the recidivism statistics for this group. In the results, a "contact" sexual offence involves actually touching a child, whereas a "noncontact" sexual offence involves an invitation, either in person or online, to sexual activity.

| TYPE OF RE-OFFENCE | NUMBER | PERCENTAGE |
|---|---|---|
| Contact sexual re-offence | 3 | 1.3 |
| Noncontact sexual re-offence | 12 | 5.3 |
| Child pornography re-offence | 10 | 4.4 |

These numbers are very low. Maybe some offences went undetected, which would push the totals higher; but remember that the subjects had all been convicted at least once of child pornography offences and were on the Ontario Sex Offender Registry and thus subject to heightened scrutiny by police. It is also true that the study was limited in time; part of the group was followed for two years and another part for five years. No doubt there would be more offences recorded if the subjects could be followed for twenty or thirty years. But no matter what qualifications are added, the conclusion from this very careful Canadian study is that many voyeurs of child pornography are not likely to commit actual offences against real children. American research, by the way, has also found that the recidivism rate for sexual offenders is lower than for any other crime except murder.

Seto and his associates offer a balanced interpretation of their data:

> Individuals who seek out child pornography are exhibiting their sexual interest in children in illegal behavior, but some of these individuals may not have the characteristics generally associated with a willingness or ability to engage in more serious illegal behavior involving direct contact with a victim who may show distress, resist, or disclose the sexual contact, resulting in severe personal and legal consequences.

In simpler language, people who commit offences against other people are usually characterized by low self-control, lack of concern for others, and impulsiveness. Only a minority of child pornography users seems to have the personality characteristics that would drive them to more serious offences.

Of course, many things can be true at the same time. The child pornography offenders in the Seto study had a lower risk of re-offending than one might have expected, given the moral panic over child pornography, but their risk was not zero. At 7 per cent for combined risk of contact and noncontact sex offences against children, it is probably much higher than the risk would be among a random sample of adult Canadian males. Interest in child pornography is indeed a risk factor for committing sexual offences against children, just as smoking is a risk factor for cancer. But we know for certain that most smokers will not die of cancer; and we can say, though not with the same certainty, that many of those who view child pornography will not commit other sexual offences against children.

More accurate predictions can be made by adding in other risk factors. A smoker whose familial ancestors had a high incidence of cancer will be at even greater risk. Similarly, a viewer of child pornography who has other anti-social characteristics will be at greater risk of committing many types of crime, including sexual assaults against children. Developing such predictive models for sexual offences is a growth industry in current child pornography research. But human variability being so great, prediction is likely to remain uncertain. Suppose we could predict, based on a number of indicators, that a specific group of men had a probability of 33 per cent of committing a sexual offence within the next five years. That figure of 33 per cent is enormously higher than the likelihood that Canadian men chosen at random would offend; and yet a 33 per cent probability of offending means than non-offending is twice as likely as offending, even among this high-risk group.

How far do we want to go down the path of preventive detention based on estimated probability of offending? This is not a hypothetical question. The Adam Walsh Act, passed in the United States in 2006, provides for civil commitment of sex offenders *after* they have served their full terms, if they are deemed to have "serious difficulty in refraining from sexually violent conduct or child molestation if released." An article in *The New Yorker* in early 2013 described how thousands of men are now in a kind of limbo in special prisons or prison wings, having served their criminal sentences but now undergoing therapy under the aegis of civil commitment. About a third of these men have been convicted only of possessing child pornography.

Although American federal law does not have a mandatory minimum sentence for simple possession of child pornography, actual sentencing practices are incredibly harsh because the sentencing grid takes account of all sorts of other factors that increase culpability. Sentences for first offences are now in the range of eight to twelve years, depending on number and type of images discovered, degree of file-sharing, and so on. Considering that civil commitment comes on top of this, it is no exaggeration to say that many child pornography voyeurs may be looking at life in prison.

Canada lagged somewhat behind the United States in adopting harsh measures against child pornography because the Mulroney government, preoccupied with major fiscal and constitutional files, did not legislate until 1993. But Canada has been moving in the same general direction as the United States, passing special legislation for child pornography, creating sex offender registries, and making penalties more severe than for other crimes. The United States, however, has reached a point where counter-pressure is beginning to build. In April 2013, the United States Sentencing Commission, an advisory body established by Congress, released a major report on sentencing practices for child pornography. While far from calling for decriminalization, the report did suggest that sentences for child pornography were getting out of hand and should be revised to reflect real danger to children, not hypothetical concerns and moral panic. The federal

Department of Justice wrote a letter of concurrence with the commission's report.

There is now at least the beginning of rational public discussion in the United States about how to deal with child pornography voyeurs. Judging from what happened to me in the Incident, Canada has not reached that point yet. Maybe we will have to have more years of ever harsher laws before a reaction will set in.

## Final Thoughts

Even though our laws about child pornography are grounded in the 1980s moral panics over satanic cults in daycare centres, repressed memory syndrome, and pedophile rings, the problem itself is real. The combination of the Internet with digital photographic technology has made images of child sexuality more readily available, at lower cost, than ever before. There is no longer much of a commercial industry in child pornography; it is mainly a matter of P2P file sharing. Files are generated and swapped all over the world, often in countries that are tolerant of child pornography and have no effective laws against it. The web really is worldwide, which makes prohibition and enforcement extremely difficult. So everyone is right to be concerned.

But concern is only the first step toward creating effective public policy. Legislating in a mood of panic is likely to create new victims without addressing the real issues. Expertise has to come into play. At this point, I'm the first to admit that I'm not an expert on sexual offences and never will be; I was dragged into the field by others who were seeking to undermine my academic and political reputation. But I have now read enough about it to be convinced that, in a laudable desire to protect our children, Canada has gone too far in the direction of trying to regulate personal conduct. Our child pornography law covers too many types of material, does not adequately distinguish between natural adolescent sexuality and pathological desires for pre-pubescent children, and imposes penalties that are too harsh on offenders whose offences take place only in the mind.

Of course, we must remember the child victims of sexual predators and try to minimize the number of such offences, but we should also take care not to create new classes of victims. I am still haunted by a heart-rending email I received shortly after the Incident; it was written by the wife of an American man imprisoned for possession of child pornography:

> I wanted to write you and let you know that I support what you said and it was not until recently that looking or sharing a picture of anything became a felony. Some people actually believe that the picture starts the crime, whereas in most cases it is the molester wanting a reward and a keepsake of what they have done.
>
> My husband is serving seven years in a US Federal Prison. He was originally charged with a crime that carried 20 to life. He had four pictures on a sharing site. In return for a guilty plea he was dropped to a lesser charge of receipt and

distribution and was able to get out on bond so he could seek therapy. He had no email evidence that he was interested in child porn or anything else, like the other people had.

In the States we have a registry and people can look you up and actually hunt you down. There are only certain places you can live and far too many sex offenders are homeless. I fear for his life in prison and even more when he comes home. The humiliation from neighbors, vandalism and even murders are not unheard of for those on the registry. Most nursing homes will not allow a sex offender to reside there and now talk of not allowing offenders who can qualify for food assistance to receive it. They will starve. My husband was sentenced to lifetime supervision, and will never be free.

I just wanted to let you know that there are people with your beliefs and understand that by what you said you are not condoning sexual abuse of children. During the time between our raid and the sentencing my husband went to therapy where he found out he had been molested from the age of two to 14. His brother, who is 10 years older, was the molester. The brother walked into federal court and admitted it, no statute of limitations, and the US Attorney did not want to prosecute. My husband was looking at the porn to try to find a young boy who was initiating sex with someone older, since he truly believed he had done that and was born with this. He had located a man through a contact on an adult porn site. He believed through conversations with this man that he may have been born this way. My husband kept being deleted from the site since he did not participate. My husband was panicked since he felt he must meet this other man and speak with him of his childhood. Due to that panic of the loss of contact, my husband kept trying to rejoin and post other people's older pictures in hopes they would not notice. My husband had no pictures of his own. My husband tells me he is now free, but at what cost? He knows that the abuse that he did not remember poisoned his thought process, but in some ways saved his life. Had he actually realized this abuse (sexual, verbal and physical) was caused by the only person he thought loved him in his family, he probably would have taken his life. The victims of today will be the sex offenders tomorrow. Over 90 percent of offenders never re-offend after being arrested, mostly due to finally getting answers that having been sought out before an arrest would have landed them in prison anyway. My husband is serving more time than most hands-on offenders.

Speaking out brings injustice to light, and I thank you.

Canadian law on child pornography is not yet that harsh, but we have been moving in that direction. I hope we can stop and reflect about what we are doing before we needlessly ruin more lives.

## CHAPTER 8

# THE FUTURE OF FREE SPEECH

FREE SPEECH IS NOT OUR NATURAL ESTATE. WE all have impulses to silence people we regard as dangerous, disagreeable, or simply inconvenient. Free speech cannot exist long without an infrastructure of laws and social conventions to keep it alive. The conventions are just as important as the laws because inconvenient speech can be silenced by social ostracism and reprisals as surely as by legal enforcement. With that in mind, let's see what the Incident can teach us about free speech in contemporary Canada. There is in fact an abundance of lessons, which fall into two distinct groups: those that mainly apply to professors and politicians and the interrelationship between the academy and government; and those regarding the speed-up of the media cycle and the rise of social media, which apply much more widely.

## Professors and Politicians

Scientists and scholars usually write for academic journals and books published by university presses and scientific publishers. As long as they stay on their home turf, so to speak, they are of little concern to politicians (here I'm referring not just to elected politicians but also to leaders of interest and advocacy groups). Politicians are engaged in building coalitions in order to influence or get control of government, so they can tailor public policy to their liking while rewarding supporters and punishing opponents. Politicians care about theoretical ideas and scientific findings mainly to the extent that they can use them as props in their endless drama of competition for political power.

Politicians care a great deal, however, about the mass media because the media are their natural playground. That's where they communicate with large numbers of people in order to build their coalitions of supporters while trying to weaken competing coalitions. They will opportunistically endorse or condemn ideas that get reported in the mass media if they see political advantage in doing so. They will not enter into scientific or scholarly debate, of which they usually have little understanding; they will use the rhetorical devices that are the stock in trade of political life.

In the *Rhetoric*, Aristotle made a classic analysis of persuasion in public life:

Of the modes of persuasion furnished by the spoken word there are three kinds. The first kind depends on the personal character of the speaker [*ethos*]; the second on putting the audience into a certain frame of mind [*pathos*]; the third on the proof, or apparent proof, provided by the words of the speech itself [*logos*]. Persuasion is achieved by the speaker's personal character when the speech is so spoken as to make us think him more credible. . . . Secondly, persuasion may come through the hearers, when the speech stirs their emotions. . . . Thirdly, persuasion is effected through the speech itself when we have proved a truth or an apparent truth by means of the persuasive arguments suitable to the case in question.

Scientists and scholars, when they are true to their calling, argue mainly by *logos,* that is, logic and evidence. Politicians rely much more on arousing emotion (*pathos*) and making arguments about character and credibility (*ethos*). For the scientist or scholar who wanders into the political line of fire, it's like being transported to a different planet.

On at least three recent occasions, Canadian politicians have provided highly publicized examples of seizing hold of an intellectual debate for political purposes. First was the Jan Wong affair of 2006. Wong was a prominent *Globe and Mail* reporter and the author of several widely read books. Her newspaper sent her to Montreal to cover the Dawson College shooting that took place on September 13, 2006. Kimveer Gill, not even a student at the college, shot twenty people (fortunately only one died), then took his own life. At the request of her employers and with subsequent editorial approval, Wong inserted a personal perspective in her essay about the events, entitled "Get Under the Desk": "What many outsiders don't realize is how alienating the decades-long linguistic struggle has been in the once-cosmopolitan city. It hasn't just taken a toll on long-time anglophones, it's affected immigrants, too."

Wong went on to draw comparisons between the Dawson shooter, Kimveer Gill, an anglophone Sikh; Valery Fabrikant, a Russian immigrant professor who shot colleagues at Concordia University; and Marc Lépine, who murdered fourteen women at the University of Montreal's École Polytechnique, and who, in spite of his francophone name, was half Algerian and had originally been named Gamil Gharbi. Wong concluded provocatively:

> To be sure, the shootings in all three cases were carried out by mentally disturbed individuals. But what is also true is that in all three cases, the perpetrator was not *pure laine*, the argot for a "pure" francophone. Elsewhere, to talk of racial "purity" is repugnant. Not in Quebec.

Throughout francophone Quebec, bloggers and mainstream media rushed to denounce her. In a September 19 letter to *The Globe and Mail*, Quebec premier Jean Charest called Wong's article a "disgrace" and demanded an apology to the people of Quebec. Prime Minister Stephen Harper piled on, writing to the *Globe* that Wong's "argument is patently absurd and without foundation . . . grossly irresponsible." On September 20, the House of Commons unanimously endorsed Liberal

MP Denis Coderre's motion calling for an apology to the people of Quebec, though the resolution did not specify whether Jan Wong or the *Globe* should apologize. Three prominent politicians from three different parties seized opportunities to pose as the defender of Quebec. They used typical political tactics of personal denunciation, demand for an apology, and parliamentary resolution, as if truth could be determined by voting. Tellingly, none bothered to engage Wong in rational debate, even though that would not have been hard to do. Her sample of three episodes was, after all, a small basis from which to draw sweeping conclusions. For her part, Wong could have replied with a lot of other evidence, both historical and contemporary, of xenophobic traits in Quebec culture. Maybe she exaggerated the consequences, but the point she had made was not far-fetched. It would have been a worthwhile debate.

At first the *Globe* defended Wong and never did apologize, but a few days later Edward Greenspon wrote in the editor's weekly column that "in hindsight, the paragraphs were clearly opinion and not reporting and should have been removed from the story" and that "the editorial quality control process sometimes breaks down on tight deadlines during grueling weeks."

Ironically, the reaction to Wong's story suggests she had a valid point. She was subjected to tons of abusive mail, including plausible death threats. Although she had been born and had grown up in Montreal, she was repeatedly attacked in the Quebec media as an Oriental outsider. *Le Devoir,* the *soi-disant* intellectual leader of francophone Quebec society, published a cartoon caricature of Wong with exaggerated buckteeth, the

Oriental equivalent of the Jewish hooked nose. It was almost as if the Québécois were trying to prove that there was some truth in what she had written. And, indeed, the proof continues to this day: think of the recent attempts of the Quebec Soccer Federation to prevent Muslim girls wearing headscarves and Sikh boys wearing turbans from playing in soccer leagues.

The second example came in 2010 when *Maclean's* published an investigation of corruption in Quebec. On the cover of the issue was a picture of the iconic Quebec snowman "Bonhomme" with a suitcase full of money. Alongside was the caption "The most corrupt province in Canada." Quebec premier Jean Charest wrote a letter denouncing *Maclean's* "twisted form of journalism and ignorance," and the House of Commons gave unanimous support to a Bloc Québécois motion: "That this House, while recognizing the importance of vigorous debate on subjects of public interest, expresses its profound sadness at the prejudice displayed and the stereotypes employed by Maclean's magazine to denigrate the Quebec nation, its history and its institutions." *Maclean's* editors stood by their story, saying their critics had not presented any evidence to refute their claims; but Rogers Media, which owns the magazine, stepped into the breach with an apology. It all seems bizarre now. After the startling revelations of the Charbonneau Commission, the arrest of two mayors and the resignation of others, and multiple police raids on local government offices, no one doubts that Quebec's problems with corruption are the worst in the country. Yet in 2010 politicians rushed to deny the obvious, brandishing insults instead of offering arguments.

And then there was my case, in which the Prime Minister's Office, the premier of Alberta, and the leader of the Official Opposition in Alberta swarmed me for questioning whether everyone convicted of possessing child pornography should automatically be sent to jail. Again, it was carried out not with rational argument but in the political language of denunciation: "It turned my stomach . . . no language strong enough to condemn . . . repugnant, ignorant, and appalling. . . ." It is no accident, I think, that all of these strident denunciations came from politicians of the right, for it is conservatives who have invested most heavily in exploiting the moral panic over child pornography, even though that panic was started by the feminist left. Conservative politicians could not stand idly by while someone with conservative credentials of his own raised questions about an issue that they had repeatedly used to attract supporters. They had to take advantage of the opportunity to reaffirm their self-appointed role as the protectors of our threatened children.

Moral panic is particularly conducive to the political seizure of debate. Moral panic leaves no room for the clash of contrasting points of view. Hyperbolic denunciation of folk devils takes the place of reasoned debate. It is a perfect setting for politicians to jump in with their slogans and catch phrases, to protect their coalitions, or even add new supporters by demonstrating their opposition to the sinister forces that threaten the community.

When ranking politicians act this way, using the executive power of the state to denounce researchers and writers, they do not set up a legal regime of censorship, but they raise the price of exercising freedom of speech. Blindside attacks by the prime minister and provincial premiers damage the reputation and livelihood of anyone engaged in the public forum. As demonstrated in my case, other public agencies take their cue from political leaders and ostracize the target, thereby compounding the damage.

I see little chance that politicians will change their behaviour; it is natural to their profession, and they do not comprehend the harm they do to free debate. Indeed, they see themselves as serving the public good by denouncing unworthy ideas. If politicians can't and won't change, then it's important for those who care about ideas and debate to fight back. The editors of *Maclean's* have set a courageous example, not just in the Bonhomme case but also when they were investigated by the Canadian Human Rights Commission for publishing an excerpt from Mark Steyn's book *America Alone*. Accused of Islamophobia, they refused to apologize; they fought back so effectively that the investigation was dropped. Indeed, their resistance, along with the efforts of Ezra Levant and others, ultimately led to passage of a private member's bill repealing section 13, which banned discriminatory telecommunications, from the Canadian Human Rights Act – a small but worthwhile political and legal victory for freedom of speech.

Universities, too, need to show more determination. With the decline of private scholars and scientists, universities are now the main repositories of learning in modern society. They, above all, should be alert to defend their members who come under political attack. It is particularly hard to do when the politicians doing the attacking are also the ones that control university funding, but academic freedom will be jeopardized if it is not done. Universities should push back publicly when politicians call for professors to be fired. University presidents should speak up as a group and demand answers from political leaders who allow or encourage their followers to engage in such attacks. Universities have to realize that academic freedom means more than not firing controversial staff members; it means defending them in the face of all sorts of reprisals, including the withdrawal of speaking invitations, termination of consulting contracts, and cancellation of publishing opportunities. Such reprisals – all of which happened to me – mean much more than the loss of a little extra income; they strike at the university professor's ability to share his research and reflection with the public. They are a means of restricting free speech without actually legislating a regime of censorship.

At the 2013 annual meeting of the Canadian Political Science Association, there was much talk about how younger political scientists are focusing on specialized research and staying away from commentary on public affairs, to the detriment of public life in Canada. Michael Byers, a University of British Columbia political scientist who is active in the NDP, was reported as saying that many scholars are reluctant to take part in public life, being afraid that what they say in public might hurt their academic careers. If my Incident is any indication, that's a realistic fear. Universities, I believe, have to take stronger steps to reassure faculty members that they will not face academic reprisals for taking part in public affairs.

## Media Madness

Today's media scene is profoundly different from what prevailed fifty years ago when I was a university student. At that time, large cities might be served by two or three local newspapers, which competed for readers and advertisers in that metropolitan area. Most newspapers did not really compete with the two or three TV stations broadcasting in the same area. Weekly newsmagazines were also important; I remember when I was a teenager starting to become interested in public affairs, how I looked forward to seeing *Newsweek* or *Time* each week so I could understand what was going on. News time was measured in days and weeks, not minutes and hours.

The situation today is infinitely more competitive, even though many newspapers have gone out of business. National newspapers, such as *The New York Times* and *Wall Street Journal* in the United States, and the *National Post* and *The Globe and Mail* in Canada, have printing facilities across the country and compete with local papers in their local media markets. Newspapers now also have to compete directly with TV stations because both types of media have their own websites where stories are posted as they appear. TV websites post summaries of their reports that read like newspaper stories, and newspaper websites post videos that look like TV reports. Indeed, they are usually actual TV stories because newspaper and TV chains are often jointly owned.

Competition is no longer confined to local media markets. Using the Internet, anyone can access any newspaper or TV station anytime, anywhere. Each morning I read the two newspapers that are delivered to my home. The rest of the day, I frequently check a news aggregator, which gives effective access to every major media outlet in Canada. When I'm interested in American news, I can get similar results by going to the Real Clear Politics website.

The combination of intense competition and new technology has produced the twenty-four-hour news cycle. Stories are posted online as soon as they are written. If one outlet has a good story, competitors will be chasing it within the hour. The concept of a daily printed newspaper is increasingly obsolete. I'm not sure why I still subscribe; I guess it's just because I'm used to reading printed papers at breakfast time. The nightly news broadcast is also becoming an anachronism. Viewers may still find it convenient to sit down and watch the news at 9 or 10 p.m., but they are unlikely to see anything that hasn't already been extensively reported during the day.

In some ways, competition and new technology have produced a Golden Age of media. More news and commentary is available more quickly, from more sources, than ever before. For anyone who cares to be well informed about public affairs, it is infinitely easier than it was even twenty-five years ago. But Golden Ages are never entirely golden, and the speed-up has come with a cost. Scott Pelley said that it is more important to be right than to be fast, but in practice being fast carries a greater reward. Fact-checking is now mostly a quaint practice of a dimly remembered past age. Media rely largely on competitors to ferret out any mistakes they may have made; after all, online stories can be corrected almost instantly if an error comes to light. That is fine, up to a point; but what about someone's reputation that may have been trashed in the first version of the story? It is always the first blast of news that makes the biggest impact. How many readers and listeners look for later corrections?

Even if outright error is not involved, the speed-up leaves little time for reflection and lends itself to "gotcha" moments that can be easily packaged in a news report. Think about the incident that happened to me. I had been teaching at a Canadian university for forty-five years. I was the author of numerous books, several of which had won prizes. I had been involved in political life for almost twenty-five years, both as an adviser to political leaders and as a commentator in the media. How plausible was it that I would suddenly announce that I was "okay with child pornography"? Even if a video with that tagline had been posted on YouTube, wouldn't common sense suggest that there was an explanation for what was portrayed in the recording? Yet without checking with me to see what I had actually meant, the media rushed to political leaders for comment, thereby creating a new and much bigger story: important people denounce Flanagan for being okay with child pornography.

Social media have exacerbated many of the effects of the Internet upon the media. They have widened the arena by making it possible for new voices to be heard. You don't have to be a journalist to post a video on YouTube. Social media force mainstream media to cover stories they might otherwise have ignored. That's probably a net advantage overall, even if some of those stories should never have been reported. And social media certainly have accelerated the speed-up even further. Newspapers and television stations now compete for stories not only against each other but against bloggers, Facebook sites, and Twitter feeds. Twitter allows politicians to post 140-character releases almost instantaneously. It all contributes to the emphasis on speed.

But there are also impacts of social media that are more dubious. For one thing, there is no editorial control. Those who post can put up whatever they want without review by another set of eyeballs. There is also no code of conduct or sense of professionalism. And then there is the impact of anonymity, the effect of which upon human behaviour has not changed since Plato talked about the ring of Gyges in the *Republic* (the ring of Gyges conferred invisibility, which arguably led to immorality). Amateurism, anonymity, and lack of editorial control make social media a swamp. Important stories are there, but how do you distinguish them from the unreliable and tendentious accounts, or even downright lies?

In my own Incident, social media became the trigger for a mainstream media massacre. Arnell Tailfeathers put up a video that was only a tiny segment of the whole evening, creating the impression that I had wanted to make a statement about child pornography. He also added an utterly misleading tagline. Treating the video as hard evidence, mainstream media then took it to politicians for reaction, without coming to me first for any context. It was the epitome of "gotcha" journalism. In this instance, social media unleashed and facilitated all the worst tendencies of mainstream media in an era when speed has become the alpha and omega of journalism.

While I was writing *Persona Non Grata* in the spring of 2013, a couple of other examples came along to illustrate the increasingly problematic role of media in public discussion.

First was the Niall Ferguson affair. Niall Ferguson is one of the best-known historians in the world. Educated at Oxford, he is now professor of history at Harvard and a fellow at the Hoover Institute and other prestigious institutions. He has written any number of best-selling books, several of which were also presented as BBC specials. He has not worked directly in politics, but he is in great demand as a speaker and consultant. Yet he also has many enemies in the left-leaning world of the academy and media because he is a self-confessed admirer of Margaret Thatcher and he publicly supported presidential candidates John McCain in 2008 and Mitt Romney in 2012 against Barack Obama.

Ferguson got into trouble while addressing a conference of financial advisers in Carlsbad, California, in early May 2013. When asked a question about economist John Maynard Keynes, he responded as follows (no transcript was published, so I quote the widely circulated report from *Financial Advisor* magazine):

> Ferguson asked the audience how many children Keynes had. He explained that Keynes had none because he was a homosexual and was married to a ballerina, with whom he likely talked of "poetry" rather than procreated. The audience went quiet at the remark. Some attendees later said they found the remarks offensive.

It gets worse.

Ferguson, who is the Laurence A. Tisch Professor of History at Harvard University, and author of *The Great Degeneration: How Institutions Decay and Economies Die,* says it's only logical that Keynes would take this selfish world-view because he was an "effete" member of society. Apparently, in Ferguson's world, if you are gay or childless, you cannot care about future generations nor society.

When the news of Ferguson's comments was published, there was a storm of criticism in the media, so Ferguson published a long and thoughtful "Open Letter to the Harvard Community" in the student newspaper. It began with a ritual apology, which was the only paragraph that I have seen cited in the press coverage:

> Last week I said something stupid about John Maynard Keynes. Asked to comment on Keynes' famous observation "In the long run we are all dead," I suggested that Keynes was perhaps indifferent to the long run because he had no children, and that he had no children because he was gay. This was doubly stupid. First, it is obvious that people who do not have children also care about future generations. Second, I had forgotten that Keynes' wife Lydia miscarried.

That seemed to settle things as far as the media were concerned. Ferguson had committed the sin of homophobia, but he had publicly recanted, so now they could go on to the next story. Pity no one seemed to read the rest of Ferguson's open letter, which talked about how he had treated Keynes and other gay men in his various writings. He also insisted, as many other scholars have done, that Keynes's sexual preferences actually did have an impact on his economic theorizing.

Keynes's story is a complex one. When he was a student at Cambridge, he joined the Apostles, a secret society many of whose members practised what they called "the higher sodomy." It was a hyper-masculine environment marked by disdain for women, repudiation of conventional morality, and glorification of male homosexuality and pederasty (Keynes, who according to his diary seduced boys as young as sixteen, would be a sex offender under today's legislation). After graduation, Keynes, like several other Apostles, became a member of the Bloomsbury Circle, which continued the same narcissistic and libertine practices. Keynes later wrote about himself and his friends at this period:

> We entirely repudiated a personal liability on us to obey general rules. We claimed the right to judge every individual case on its merits, and the wisdom to do so successfully. This was a very important part of our faith, violently and aggressively held, and for the outer world it was our most obvious and dangerous characteristic. We repudiated entirely customary morals, conventions and traditional wisdom. We were, that is to say, in the strict sense of the term, immoralists.

Keynes, like Karl Marx, studied philosophy at university and only later became a self-taught economist. Just as anyone who wants to understand Marx has to know something about his philosophical inheritance from Hegel, anyone who wants to understand Keynes has to know something about the philosophical ideas on which he was nourished. The crucial thing about Keynes was not his homosexuality but his rejection of what George Bernard Shaw satirized as "middle class morality," including the Victorian virtues of marital fidelity, self-discipline, and thrift. That's directly connected to Keynes's views about the danger of the liquidity trap and the virtues of government deficit finance in times of depression.

This is not just the academic chatter of intellectual historians. There has been a revival of Keynesianism in the wake of the Great Recession of 2008, with prominent writers such as Paul Krugman, a Nobel Prize–winning economist and *New York* Times columnist, advocating unprecedented levels of deficit spending. Anyone interested in the Keynesian revival should also know something about the intellectual matrix of Keynes's ideas on deficit spending.

Niall Ferguson committed a faux pas and was justly reproved. He took an intellectual shortcut in trying to illustrate the problems in Keynesianism, which made him seem engaged in a kind of intellectual gay-bashing. His faux pas, however, could have become one of what President Obama calls "teachable moments," if the media had shown the slightest interest in the very important issues surrounding Keynes's economic doctrines and their ethical background. Sadly but predictably, the media preferred to deal with the story as kabuki theatre, featuring a mock drama of offence and apology.

I leave the last word to Ferguson:

In the long run we are all indeed dead, at least as individuals. Perhaps Keynes was lucky to pre-decease the bloggers because, for all his brilliance, was also prone to moments of what we would now call political incorrectness. In his Economic Consequences of the Peace, for example, he wrote: "Unless her great neighbours are prosperous and orderly, Poland is an economic impossibility with no industry but Jew-baiting." Even at the time, that was an outrageous thing to say about a country that had suffered grave hardships since its partition in the eighteenth century. But does anyone today seriously argue that we should not read Keynes because he was a Polonophobe?

Ironically, Keynes was even more averse to Americans than to Poles. As he told a friend in 1941: "I always regard a visit [to the US] as in the nature of a serious illness to be followed by convalescence." To his eyes, Washington was dominated by lawyers, all speaking incomprehensible legalese – or, as Keynes put it, "Cherokee".

Shock, horror: Even the mighty Keynes occasionally said stupid things. Most professors do. And – let's face it – so do most students.

What the self-appointed speech police of the blogosphere forget is that to err occasionally is an integral part of the learning process. And one of the things I learnt from my stupidity last week is that those who seek to demonize error, rather than forgive it, are among the most insidious enemies of academic freedom.

From the rarefied circles of Oxford and Harvard, let's move to the political circus of Toronto politics, starring Mayor Rob Ford and his brother Doug, a city councillor. But first take a stop in New York City to learn about Gawker, a gossip blog that has been publishing for about ten years. Gawker has numerous scoops to its credit, including the story of U.S. congressman Chris Lee sending shirtless photos of himself to a woman he had met on Craigslist. Gawker is part of new media, in the sense that it is paperless, but it is not part of social media; it is a highly successful business competing with more traditional tabloids and gossip columns.

On May 16, 2013, Gawker published an article by editor-in-chief John Cook claiming he had gone to Toronto to see a cellphone video of Rob Ford puffing on a crack pipe. Ford also reportedly made derogatory comments about gays and racial minorities while smoking cocaine. The video, made within the last six months, was being offered for sale by a drug dealer for $200,000. Gawker doesn't have that kind of money, however, so it set up a crowd-sourcing site for people to make donations and raised the full amount within two weeks.

Since Gawker did not have a copy of the video, it enlivened the original story with a photograph of Mayor Ford with three young black men. One of them, Anthony Smith, had been recently killed in a gangland shooting, and the other two were arrested in June 2013 as part of Project Traveller, a police investigation of drug and gun dealing. Gawker reported that the photo had been taken while Ford was on the cocaine-buying trip that led to the video.

Gawker's story in itself might have had limited impact in Canada; after all, it was published in a gossip blog in another country. But the *Toronto Star* published the same picture on May 17, together with a report about the video, claiming the tipster trying to sell the video had made the photo available. According to the *Star*'s reporters, they had been talking to the Somali drug dealers for weeks before they got to see the video. The *Star* is the largest-circulation newspaper in Canada and certainly the leader in coverage of Toronto metropolitan news. Its story touched off a media storm that was still ongoing at the time of my final deadline for revisions (November 2013).

Things came to a head on Halloween, when the Toronto police announced they had recovered a copy of the video of Ford smoking a crack pipe but would not release it now because it would later be needed as evidence in court. Police Chief Bill Blair described the contents as "disappointing." The same day, Ford's friend and sometime driver, Sandro Lisi, who had been arrested three weeks earlier for trafficking in marijuana, was charged with extortion in connection with having tried to retrieve the video.

On November 7, the *Toronto Star* posted another video on its website, which it had purchased for $5,000. It showed Rob Ford raging in what appeared to be an empty dining room, shouting semi-coherently about killing someone. The context is unknown, as is the identity of whoever made the video.

I can't possibly do justice to the whole Rob Ford story; that would require a book in itself. I just want to comment on the role of new technology and new media in the unfolding of the story.

Private photography and video recording with small, inexpensive devices were absolutely crucial. They had far more impact than if they had been delivered by mere rumours or even eyewitness reports of the mayor abusing drugs, but they differ in the extent to which they were invasions of individual privacy. The photo of Ford with the three young men must have been consensual because he posed for it with his arms around them. The video of Ford smoking a crack pipe seems to have been surreptitious, but it is hard to be outraged because the mayor was breaking the Criminal Code. I'm not a lawyer, but I don't think a person, especially an elected politician of high rank, can reasonably expect that a video of him committing a crime in the presence of other people will remain forever concealed.

The second video, however, is more troubling from the standpoint of privacy. Ford seems to have been drunk, and he was spouting off about harming and even killing someone, though the violent language may have been metaphorical. It didn't look to me like the kind of threat that could be considered criminal. A drunken fit of bad temper in which no one is injured is not an advertisement of good character but neither is it illegal. It augurs poorly for privacy if a surreptitious recording of such a temper tantrum is considered fair game for sale to the media. Big Brother may not always be watching you, but you sure have to be on the lookout for "friends" with cellphones.

The case of Rob Ford is, of course, quite different from mine. He apparently broke the law by using cocaine; I was pilloried for questioning aspects of the law on child pornography. But there are some important similarities in the role of the media. In both cases, frenzy in the mainstream media was triggered by an electronic posting – of a video clip on YouTube in my case, of a story about a video on a gossip blog in Rob Ford's case. In both instances, the existence of a video was widely taken as incontrovertible proof, despite dodgy circumstances – a tendentious tagline in my case, absence of the video in Rob Ford's case.

Indeed, the circumstances surrounding the Rob Ford video cried out for journalistic caution. The video when first reported was unavailable to the public and could not be authenticated. It was offered for sale for a large amount of money by self-avowed drug dealers, who disappeared even though Gawker raised enough money to buy it. The video could have been evidence in a criminal investigation, of both using and selling illegal drugs. Is it even legal to sell such evidence? If the video was made by the seller of the drugs, he would be trying to benefit financially from his crime, which is illegal in the United States, where money was raised to buy it. It was almost yellow journalism, fare for tabloid scandal sheets, yet it was reported and hugely discussed in Canada's largest and most respectable media outlets. Even though the police now say they have recovered and authenticated the video (it still hasn't been shown to the public), the way it was first reported gives cause for concern.

What should be done about the contemporary media madness? One thing is certain: these are not problems that can be solved by government. State regulation of media is a sure way to stifle rather than enhance freedom of speech and discussion. What is needed, rather, is an improved set of journalistic conventions to guide reporting in the age of the twenty-four-hour news cycle.

Think of what happened in North America in the twentieth century. At the beginning of the century, the news media – newspapers, really – were in poor shape. Many were rabidly partisan, even owned by politicians, others belonged to the category of sensationalist yellow press, like the newspaper empire of William Randolph Hearst, the model for Orson Welles's famous film *Citizen Kane*. It was a raucous time of adjustment to new political conditions – mass democracy – and new technology – high-speed printing presses.

Over the course of the century, however, the industry improved itself through many different initiatives – establishment of schools of journalism, fellowships and prizes for high journalistic achievement, adoption of codes of professional ethics, creation of in-house review processes. The ideal of responsible, objective news coverage emerged as the goal of journalism, supplanting sensationalism and rabid partisanship. These unlovely twins did not disappear from the media scene, but they ceased to dominate it.

We are again at a time of major technological and political change, with the proliferation of new media and the globalization of politics. I believe conventions, including business practices and ethical standards, will have to evolve to fit the new realities. I am neither a journalist nor an expert on media, so I can't say exactly what these new conventions will be; they will have to emerge through the experience of those who work in the industry. But I can point out some current practices that need attention, because they are penalizing freedom of speech and degrading democratic debate. My list would include:

- "Gotcha" journalism that takes statements out of context to create pseudo-moralistic dramas of offence and repentance;
- Emphasis on statements that contradict someone's code of political correctness;
- Regarding video as proof of events without regard to provenance and context;
- Reliance on new media and social media, despite the absence of professional standards;
- Reliance on anonymous sources;
- And, above all, extreme emphasis on speed, to the detriment of fact-checking and thoughtful analysis.

The importance of conventions is illustrated by the case of Dr. Benjamin Levin, a professor of education at the University of Toronto and former deputy minister of education in Manitoba and Ontario. In July 2013, Dr. Levin was arrested by police and charged with making pornographic images available, creating child pornography through the written word, advising another person on how to commit sexual assault upon a child, and arranging for a sexual assault upon a child to take place.

Lesser charges of possessing and accessing child pornography were added later.

I have no idea what Dr. Levin may or may not have done, and we probably won't know until these very serious charges are tried in court. Here I simply want to draw attention to the way these allegations were treated by politicians and reported in the media.

Levin was closely connected to leading Liberal politicians; indeed, he was photographed at the 2013 Toronto Gay Pride parade sitting next to Ontario Premier Kathleen Wynne, federal Liberal leader Justin Trudeau, and former Liberal leader Bob Rae. Levin had previously been deputy minister of education while Wynne was minister, and he had also served in 2013 on her transition team after she won the provincial Liberal leadership race and became premier of Ontario. In view of this close association, Premier Wynne had to say something, but her statement was a model of restraint, compared with what politicians said about me:

> I was shocked to hear about these charges through the news on Monday. Insidious crimes like these are absolutely terrifying. The safety and well-being of our children has always been my absolute priority, and at no time did I have any suspicion of criminal behavior. I am confident that the police and judicial system will address these serious allegations.

Minister of Education Liz Sandals also made a restrained statement about Levin, who had been doing various kinds of work for the department:

He has been on contract research projects and guest speaking roles – work that has been suspended pending the outcome of the investigation. As these allegations are currently before the courts and the subject of an ongoing police investigation – the integrity of which must be protected – it would be inappropriate for the ministry to comment at this time.

And that was about all. Other politicians did not rush to pile on; they simply said nothing in public. The University of Toronto asked him to take leave from his duties while the charges against him were pending and issued this relatively restrained statement:

Recently, charges were laid against Professor Benjamin Levin of the Ontario Institute for Studies in Education (OISE). The charges against Professor Levin are extremely serious. The University understands that an individual is innocent until proven guilty. In this case the gravity of the charges in relation to the mission of OISE is such that Professor Levin has ceased all University activities at this time.

Reports in the media were also cautious. The arrest was covered as a news story, but it was not hyped on front pages across the country. Conservative columnists Michael Coren and Ezra Levant suggested that Levin had been responsible for the rather explicit sex education curriculum withdrawn by Premier Dalton McGuinty under popular pressure, but Premier Wynne denied that Levin had been involved in drafting the curriculum. And that was about it for media commentary. All in all, unless you lived in Toronto, you wouldn't have heard much about the whole thing without searching the Internet.

Why was the political and media response to the Levin incident so different from what happened in my Incident? Some friends have suggested that the media went easier on Levin because he was a Liberal, but I'm not convinced. That might explain the behaviour of some Toronto news outlets, but not of Conservative-leaning media such as the *National Post*, CanWest, and the *Sun* chain. I think the deeper reason is the presence of criminal charges in the equation. Canadian politicians and media commentators are traditionally wary of piling on when matters are before the courts, particularly in criminal cases.

Importantly, very little of this self-restraint comes from black-letter law. The doctrines of separation of powers and judicial independence make up a constitutional backdrop for elected politicians, but there is nothing explicit in the written constitution or in legislation telling politicians not to comment on cases while they are being tried. Judges might conceivably issue orders against media if they thought coverage was compromising the possibility of a fair trial, but that wouldn't be effective if media routinely and recklessly commented on cases under trial. No, the self-restraint of politicians and media regarding criminal trials is largely a matter of convention and tradition. Yet it is highly effective. As an American immigrant to Canada, I often reflect on how depoliticized the Canadian justice system is in comparison with that in the United States – and the difference is mainly a result of custom and culture, not legislation and constitutional law. What we need now is a broader set of conventions to guide political news reporting and commentary in the age of the twenty-four-hour news cycle.

## What Difference Does It Make?

I take it for granted that Canadians believe public affairs should be guided by truth, to the extent that our limited human minds can discover it. There's nothing I can say to those who, like Dosteyevsky's Grand Inquisitor, would base social structures on lies, except to state my conviction that there is an objective order to the world, and if we ignore it, we will pay a grievous price in the end. But if we all agree that truth is desirable, the question becomes, What is the best way for fallible human intelligence to approximate it?

The classic answer is found in John Stuart Mill's essay *On Liberty*, and I can do no better than present his argument in simplified form. Mill organized his argument in three branches to show why repression is harmful and free speech is useful.

First, assume that the authorities wish to repress what is true. That case hardly needs much discussion. If we start by assuming that the truth is useful and necessary, then it is harmful to repress it.

Second, assume that the authorities wish to establish the truth by punishing those who would challenge it. What's wrong with that? Given that we already know the truth, why waste time with questioning it? All would-be censors and mavens of political correctness would do well to memorize

Mill's answer. I quoted these words earlier in the book, and now I quote them again because they are so important:

> He who knows only his own side of the case knows little of that. His reasons may be good, and no one may have been able to refute them. But if he is equally unable to refute the reasons on the opposite side, if he does not so much as know what they are, he has no ground for preferring either opinion.

In practice, most of us trust to authority most of the time to establish what is true. I believe that the earth revolves around the sun rather than the sun around the earth, but I'm not sure I know how to prove it. What justifies my belief in what I learned from my teachers is the existence of free and open debate, in which challenge to accepted truths is possible. It is rational to believe that the earth revolves around the sun because astronomers, who specialize in such matters, can be challenged; and we would presumably hear about it if they could not answer the objections of those who think the earth is the centre of the universe.

Finally (and this applies to all the great practical issues of public life), assume that the whole truth is not clear to anyone, and that different people and factions advocate truth and false-hood mixed in unknown proportions. In that tableau, our only recourse is constant challenge and debate if we hope to winnow out the wheat from the chaff. No one knows the complete truth for certain, so no one should have the authority to declare that the time for discussion is over. If we were divine beings, we would not need freedom of speech because truth would be self-evident to our minds. But we are not divine; we are human beings whose intelligence is frail and limited. Working together through the exchange of ideas is our only hope of transcending our limitations.

This discussion is highly abstract, but it has very practical implications. Take child pornography as an example. Forty years ago, child pornography hardly existed as a separate topic of discussion. There was no special law regarding it; it was, at most, a minor part of the general category of obscenity regulated by the Criminal Code. Then came a moral panic over repressed memory syndrome, satanic cults in daycare centres, and pedophile rings, leading to specific legislation about child pornography. In itself, the panic was nothing but fantasy; but the arrival of the Internet in the 1990s created a new era of child pornography, enabling pedophiles all over the world to get together online and swap images. There is, therefore, a real and historically unprecedented question of what to do about child pornography in the age of the Internet. How do we protect our children without needlessly creating a new class of victims?

Trying to answer that question is extremely difficult. It calls for careful analysis, thoughtful reflection, examination of evidence, and continual monitoring of whatever policies are enacted to determine their real-world effects. Hysterical denunciation of those who raise doubts about this or that aspect of existing policy is exactly what we don't need. If readers of *Persona Non Grata* see this, then maybe some good can come out of the Incident after all.

# *Acknowledgements*

My greatest debt is to my wife, Marianne, and daughter, Rebecca, whose love sustained me in the darkest days of the Incident. Brenda O'Neil, Richard Sigurdson, Jack Mintz, and Sheila Miller helped in various ways to resolve my difficulties with the University of Calgary. Rick Billington provided legal advice when I needed it. Jaime Watt and Carrie Kormos gave indispensable help in coping with media. Doug Pepper offered to publish this book with McClelland & Stewart and then followed up with lots of excellent editorial advice. My thanks go out to you and to the many others mentioned in these pages who came to my assistance in so many different ways.

I also want to thank the authors – some friends, some people I had never met – who expressed their own views in the media during the Incident, including: Michael Taube, Mark Mercer, and William Watson in the *Ottawa Citizen*; Barbara Kay, Jonathan Kay, Terry Corcoran, and John von Heyking in the *National Post*; Richard French in the *Globe and Mail*; Rainer Knopff, Curtis

Eaton, and Licia Corbella in the *Calgary Herald;* Lauren Heuser on LegalEase.co.uk; Brenda Cossman in *Xtra!;* Barry Cooper in Troy Media; Conrad Black on HuffingtonPost.ca; Peter Russell on OntarioNewswatch.com; Michael Enright on *CBC Sunday Edition*; and Barbara Amiel in *Maclean's.* I list their names as an expression of gratitude. Only someone who has been through a mobbing experience can understood how important it is to have others show support.

Finally, I want to acknowledge the hundreds of people who sent messages of support by email or snail mail, who called me or my wife on the telephone, or who popped into the office for a quick word. Hearing from all of you was one of the most interesting and important experiences of my life. I can't name you all, but I think of you often.

# Sources

## INTRODUCTION

**pp. 1–2.** Philip Roth, *The Human Stain* (Boston: Houghton Mifflin, 2000). The movie of the same title was released by Miramax in 2003. Roth identified Melvin Tumin as the source for his novel in "An Open Letter to Wikipedia," http://www.newyorker.com/online/blogs/ books/2012/09/an-open-letter-to-wikipedia.html. For the story of the Washington, D.C., employee who was fired and then rehired after using the word *niggardly*, see Yolanda Woodlee, "D.C. Mayor Acted 'Hastily,' Will Rehire Aide," *Washington Post*, February 4, 1999, http://www.washingtonpost.com/wp-srv/local/longterm/williams /williams020499.htm.

**pp. 3–4.** Franz Kafka, *Metamorphosis,* trans. David Wylie, 2002, http://www.gutenberg.org/files/5200/5200-h/5200-h.htm.

**p. 4.** The Beatles, "A Little Help from My Friends," 1967; Blanche DuBois is a character in a play by Tennessee Williams, *A Streetcar Named Desire,* 1947.

**p. 6.** For more on First Nations terminology, see Tom Flanagan, *First Nations? Second Thoughts*, 2nd ed. (Montreal: McGill-Queen's University Press, 2008).

**p. 7.** Summers's speech (he spoke from notes) was reported in the *Harvard Crimson*, January 14, 2005, http://www.thecrimson.com /article/2005/1/14/summers-comments-on-women-and-science

**p. 7.** Doreen Kimura, "Sex Differences in the Brain," *Scientific American*, May 13, 2002, http://www2.nau.edu/~bio372-c/class /behavior/sexdif1.htm.

**p. 9.** Lincoln's famous formulation comes from the Gettysburg Address, November 19, 1863, http://www.d.umn.edu/~rmaclin /gettysburg-address.html.

### CHAPTER 1

**pp. 12–13.** For a more academic account of my career, see Tom Flanagan, "A Political Scientist in Public Affairs," Nelson Wiseman, ed., *The Public Intellectual in Canada* (Toronto: Toronto University Press, 2013), pp. 125–149. My publications are all available at my website http://www.tom-flanagan.ca.

**p. 13.** Eric Voegelin, *The New Science of Politics* (Chicago: University of Chicago Press, 1952); Gerhart Niemeyer, *Between Nothingness and Paradise* (Baton Rouge, LA: Louisiana State University Press, 1971).

**p. 16.** George F. G. Stanley, *Louis Riel* (Toronto: Ryerson, 1963); Norman Cohn, *The Pursuit of the Milliennium*, rev. ed. (New York: Oxford University Press, 1970).

**p. 17.** George F. G. Stanley et al., *The Collected Writings of/Les Ecrits complets de Louis Riel* (Edmonton: University of Alberta Press, 1985). Thomas Flanagan, *Louis 'David' Riel: Prophet of the New World,* rev. ed. (Toronto: University of Toronto Press, 1996); Gilles Martel, *Les Messianisme de Louis Riel* (Waterloo: Wilfrid Laurier University Press, 1984).

**p. 17.** Thomas Flanagan, *Riel and the Rebellion: 1885 Reconsidered,* 2nd. ed. (Toronto: University of Toronto Press, 2000).

**p. 18.** *Manitoba Métis Federation Inc. v. Canada (Attorney General),* 2013 SCC 14.

**p. 18.** Thomas Flanagan, *Metis Lands in Manitoba* (Calgary: University of Calgary Press, 1991).

**p. 18.** My articles on the Lubicon dispute are cited in Tom Flanagan, *Game Theory and Canadian Politics* (Toronto: University of Toronto Press, 1998), p. 176, n. 1.

**p. 19.** *Canada v. Benoit,* 2003 FCA 236 (2003); *Ermineskin Indian Band and Nation v. Canada,* 2009 SCC 9; [2009] 1 S.C.R. 222.

**p. 19.** Tom Flanagan, *First Nations? Second Thoughts,* 2nd ed. (Montreal: McGill-Queen's University Press, 2008).

**pp. 19–20.** Tom Flanagan, Christopher Alcantara, and André Le Dressay, *Beyond the Indian Act: Restoring Aboriginal Property Rights,* 2nd ed. (Montreal: McGill-Queen's University Press, 2010).

**p. 20.** Pamela D. Palmater, "Opportunity or Temptation? Plans for private property on reserves could cost First Nations their independence," *Literary Review of Canada,* http://reviewcanada.ca

/magazine/2010/04/opportunity-or-temptation/. And https://
www.facebook.com/IdleNoMoreSaskatoon/info.

**pp. 20–21.** John Stuart Mill, *On Liberty* (Indianapolis: Liberal Arts
Press, 1956), p. 45.

**p. 22.** The first book I read by Hayek was *The Constitution of Liberty*
(Chicago: University of Chicago Press, 1960). His greatest work, in
my opinion, is *Law, Legislation and Liberty*, 3 vols. (Chicago: University of Chicago Press, 1973–79).

**p. 23.** An updated edition is Tom Flanagan, *Waiting for the Wave: The
Reform Party and the Conservative Movement*, 2nd ed. (Montreal:
McGill-Queen's University Press, 2009).

**pp. 25–26.** Stephen Harper et al., "An Open Letter to Ralph Klein,"
*National Post*, January 24, 2001.

**p. 28.** Tom Flanagan, *Harper's Team: Behind the Scenes in the Conservative
Rise to Power,* 2nd ed. (Montreal: McGill-Queen's University Press, 2009).

**p. 28.** Senator Doug Finley died May 11, 2013.

**p. 31.** My original comments are on You Tube, http://www.youtube
.com/watch?v=5wLYy7ETO34.

**p. 32.** Robert Fowler, *A Season in Hell: My 130 Days in the Sahara with
Al Qaeda* (Toronto: HarperCollins, 2011).

**pp. 34–35.** I tell the story of the 2012 Wildrose campaign in *Winning
Power: Canadian Campaigning in the 21st Century* (Montreal: McGill-
Queen's University Press, 2014).

**p. 36.** Arthur J. Ray, *Telling It to the Judge: Taking Native History to Court* (Montreal: McGill-Queen's University Press, 2011).

## CHAPTER 2

**pp. 40–41.** I couldn't find Laura Blakely's recording online in August 2013 when I went back to write up the source notes. CBC News, "Tom Flanagan made child-porn comments in Manitoba in 2009," March 1, 2013, http://www.cbc.ca/news/canada/manitoba/story/2013/03/01 /mb-tom-flanagan-university-manitoba-comments.html.

**pp. 43–44.** http://www.sacpa.ca.

**p. 44.** Sue Grafton, *V is for Vengeance* (New York: Berkley Books, 2013).

**p. 45.** Shari Narine, "Strategy results further reaching than expected," *Alberta Sweetgrass,* 2013, but no further date on posting, http://www.ammsa.com/publications/alberta-sweetgrass/strategy -results-further-reaching-expected.

**pp. 47–48.** Jen Gerson's *National Post* story online contains a screen-shot of the buffalo coat, http://news.nationalpost.com/2013/01/30/ it-makes-me-an-icon-of-canadian-history-tom-flanagans-enormous- fuzzy-bison-hide-coat-causes-twitter-furor.

**pp. 48–49.** The exchange is online at http://www.youtube.com /watch?v=LqS4qKkE_SY.

**pp. 49–50.** Mill, *On Liberty,* p. 100.

**pp. 52–53.** Smith's February 28, 2013, statement is on the Wildrose website, http://www.wildrose.ca/feature/wildrose-leader-smith-condemns-flanagans-child-porn-remarks.

**p. 54.** https://twitter.com/PMO_MacDougall/status/307169930896347136.

**p. 54.** Redford quoted in http://www.cp24.com/news/flanagan-retires-from-post-after-child-porn-comments-1.1176132.

**pp. 54–55.** Ron Paul's speech explaining his vote, June 26, 2002, is online at http://www.politechbot.com/p-03690.html.

**p. 55.** The CBC statement is online at http://www.newswire.ca/en/story/1122007/cbc-news-statement-regarding-tom-flanagan.

**p. 56.** My statement is posted online at http://www.cbc.ca/news/canada/calgary/story/2013/02/28/calgary-tom-flanagan-child-porn.html.

**p. 59.** Michael Taube, "Tom Flanagan is wrong, not evil," *Ottawa Citizen*, March 1, 2013, http://www2.canada.com/ottawacitizen/news/archives/story.html?id=1e79f19c-cc2d-4a5a-a3df-ba464d841bdf&p=2.

**pp. 59–60.** Barbara Kay, "A distinguished career vanishes with the wind," *National Post*, March 1, 2013, http://fullcomment.nationalpost.com/2013/03/01/barbara-kay-a-distinguished-career-vanishes-with-the-wind.

**p. 60.** Jonathan Kay, "The mobbing of Tom Flanagan is unwarranted and cruel," *National Post*, March 1, 2013, http://fullcomment.nationalpost.com/2013/03/01/jonathan-kay-the-mobbing-of-tom-flanagan-is-unwarranted.

**p. 61.** "Tom Flanagan in his own words: Ex-Harper strategist explains controversial child-pornography comments," *National Post,* March 4, 2013, http://fullcomment.nationalpost.com/2013/03/04/tom -flanagan-in-his-own-words-ex-harper-strategist-explains-controversial -child-pornography-comments.

**p. 61.** "Tom Flanagan Responds," http://www.youtube.com/ watch?v=YSHegzqldZ4.

**pp. 61–62.** "Tom Flanagan on child pornography, the backlash and the worst week of his life," *Maclean's,* March 8, 2013, http://www2. macleans.ca/2013/03/08/on-discussing-child-porn-the-backlash- and-the-worst-week-of-his-life.

**p. 62.** Smith quoted in Dean Bennett, "Ex-Tory adviser Flanagan says he was trapped into child porn comments," *Globe and Mail,* March 4, 2013, http://www.theglobeandmail.com/news/politics/ex-tory-adviser-flana- gan-says-he-was-trapped-into-child-porn-comments/article9259987.

**p. 63.** Brenda Cossman, "Flanagan's Question Worth Discussing," *Daily Xtra,* March 4, 2013, http://dailyxtra.com/canada/ideas/edi- torial-flanagans-question-worth-discussing.

**p. 63.** Michael Enright, "Defending Tom Flanagan," *CBC Sunday Edition,* March 17, 2013, http://www.cbc.ca/thesundayedition/ essays/2013/03/17/michael-1/.

**p. 63.** Chris Plecash, "Manning stands by decision . . .," *Hill Times,* March 9, 2013, http://www.hilltimes.com/news/politics /2013/03/09/manning-stands-by-decision-to-drop-flanagan -from-manning-networking-conference/33972.

**pp. 63–64.** Licia Corbella, "Flanagan's valuable lesson," *Calgary Herald,* March 12, 2013, http://www2.canada.com/calgaryherald /news/theeditorialpage/story.html?id=63e276e8-4fed-454c-b837 -d11f03492c34&p=1.

CHAPTER 3

**p. 65.** Meredith Willson, *The Music Man,* 1957, stage play; movie 1962.

**pp. 65–66.** Stanley Cohen, *Folk Devils and Moral Panics: The Creation of the Mods and Rockers,* 3rd ed. London: Routlege, 2002). A recent compilation of research is Sean P. Hier, ed., *Moral Panic and the Politics of Anxiety* (London: Routledge, 2011).

**p. 68.** Emily F. Murphy ("Janey Canuck"), *The Black Candle* (Toronto: Thomas Allen, 1922).

**p. 69.** *Safe Streets and Communities Act,* S.C. 2012, c. 1, s. 41.1.

**p. 69.** Philip Jenkins, *Moral Panic: Changing Concepts of the Child Molester in Modern America* (New Haven: Yale University Press, 1998).

**p. 70.** Quotations from Greer, Brownmiller, and Morgan are all taken from Mark O. Dickerson, Tom Flanagan, and Brenda O'Neill, *Introduction to Government and Politics: A Conceptual Approach,* 9th ed. (Toronto: Nelson, 2013), p. 186.

**p. 71.** *Criminal Code of Canada,* s. 271.

**p. 71.** *R. v. Butler,* [1992] 1 SCR 452.

**pp. 71–72.** Doug Linder, "The McMartin Preschool Abuse Trial:

A Commentary," 2003, http://law2.umkc.edu/faculty/projects/ftrials/mcmartin/mcmartinaccount.html.

**p. 72.** Michael Edward Hale, *The Martensville Moral Panic,* M.A. thesis, University of British Columbia, Department of Anthropology, 2001, https://circle.ubc.ca/handle/2429/11542.

**pp. 74–75.** Ellen Bass and Laura Davis, *The Courage to Heal: A Guide for Women Survivors of Child Sexual Abuse* (New York: Harper & Row, 1988). Elizabeth Loftus, *The Myth of Repressed Memory: False Memories and Allegations of Sexual Abuse* (New York: St. Martin's, 1994).

**p. 76.** Robert Benzie and Rob Ferguson, "Huge inquiry fails to find ring in Cornwall," *Toronto Star,* December 16, 2009, http://www.thestar.com/news/ontario/2009/12/16/huge_inquiry_fails_to_find_pedophile_ring_in_cornwall.html.

**pp. 77–82.** Robin F. Badgley, *Sexual offences against children: report of the Committee on Sexual Offences Against Children and Youths appointed by the Minister of Justice and Attorney General of Canada, the Minister of National Health and Welfare* (1984), 2 vols.

**p. 82.** Brian Mulroney, *Memoirs: 1939-1993* (Toronto: McClelland and Stewart, 2007).

**p. 83.** Bill C-128, An Act to amend the Criminal Code and the Customs Tariff (child pornography and corrupting morals), introduced May 13, 1993. http://www3.sympatico.ca/toshiya.k.ncl/c-128/c-128final.htm.

**pp. 83–84.** *R. v. Sharpe,* BCCA [1999], 416 at para. 213.

**p. 84.** *R. v. Sharpe,* [2001] 1 SCR 45.

**p. 85.** Bill C-2, An Act to amend the Criminal Code (protection of children and other vulnerable persons) and the Canada Evidence Act, introduced October 8, 2004, http://www.parl.gc.ca/About/Parliament /LegislativeSummaries/bills_ls.asp?ls=C2&Parl=38&Ses=1.

**p. 86.** Bill C-10, Safe streets and communities Act (short title), introduced September 20, 2011, http://www.parl.gc.ca/legisinfo /BillDetails.aspx?billId=5120829&Mode=1&Language=E. Vidya Kauri, "Harper unveils plans for tougher laws against child sex offenders," *Globe and Mail,* August 29, 2013.

CHAPTER 4

**p. 88.** Kenneth Westhues, "Mobbing: A Natural Fact," posted on his webpage about mobbing: http://arts.uwaterloo.ca/~kwesthue/ mobbing.htm.

**p. 89.** Frans de Waal, *Chimpanzee Politics: Power and Sex among Apes,* rev. ed. (Baltimore, MD.: Johns Hopkins University Press, 2007). Christopher Boehm: *Moral Origins: The Evolution of Virtue, Altruism, and Shame* (New York: Basic Books, 2012).

**p. 90.** Steven Pinker, *The Better Angels of Our Nature: Why Violence Has Declined* (New York: Penguin, 2011).

**p. 91.** Maureen Duffy and Len Sperry, *Mobbing: Causes, Consequences, Solutions* (Oxford University Press, 2012).

**pp. 95–97.** Hunsperger's blog post is reprinted in *Edmonton Journal,*

April 15, 2012, http://blogs.edmontonjournal.com/2012/04/15 /wildrose-candidate-allan-hunsperger-on-gays-you-will-suffer-the -rest-of-eternity-in-the-lake-of-fire-hell.

**p. 99.** I described the 2004 campaign episode in *Harper's Team*, pp. 177- 180. Laura Payton, "Toews steps back from child pornographers comment," CBC website, February 16, 2012, http://www.cbc.ca/ news/politics/story/2012/02/16/toews-twitter-attack-house-of-com- mons.html. "Rift Threatens to Divide the Conservative Party," http://www.thecanadianencyclopedia.com/articles/macleans/rift- threatens-to-divide-the-conservative-party.

**p. 101.** Aristotle, *Nicomachean Ethics*, II, 6, 1107a.

**p. 103.** Stacy Schiff, *Cleopatra: A Life* (New York: Little Brown, 2010).

CHAPTER 5

**pp. 112–113.** http://en.wikipedia.org/wiki/The_Bottle_Deposit.

**p. 113.** http://en.wikipedia.org/wiki/The_Finale_(Seinfeld)

**p. 117.** *"Man hat der Historie das Amt, die Vergangenheit zu richten, die Mitwelt zum Nutzen zukuenftiger Jahre zu belehren, beigemessen: so hoher Aemter unterwindet sich gegenwaertiger Versuch nicht: er will blos zeigen, wie es eigentlich gewesen."* http://howitreallywas.typepad.com/how_ it_really_was/2005/10/wie_es_eigentli.html.

**pp. 117–118.** Tom Wolfe, *Back to Blood: A Novel* (New York: Little Brown and Company, 2012).

**p. 119.** Ernest Renan, "What Is a Nation?" reprinted in Mark O. Dickerson, Thomas Flanagan, and Neil Nevitte, eds., *Introductory Readings in Government and Politics,* 4th edition (Toronto: Nelson Canada, 1995), p. 21.

**pp. 120–121.** Mario Toneguzzi, "Conrad Black comes out in support of Calgary political strategist Tom Flanagan," *Calgary Herald,* May 11, 2013, http://www.calgaryherald.com/news/calgary/Conrad+Black +comes+support+Calgary+political+strategist+Flanagan/8369076 /story.html.

**p. 121.** Conrad Black, *A Matter of Principle* (New York: Encounter Books, 2012), p. 501.

**pp. 124–125.** Alexis de Tocqueville, *Democracy in America,* trans. George Lawrence (Garden City, NY: Anchor Books, 1969), Vol. 2, Part 1, Ch. 12, p. 469.

**pp. 126–127.** http://www.quinnipiac.edu/news-events/scott-pelley -cbs-evening-news-to-receive-fred-friendly-first-amendment-award -may-10.

### CHAPTER 6

**pp. 133–134.** http://www.caut.ca/issues-and-campaigns/aca- demic-freedom.

**p. 133.** Collective agreement 2011-2013, p. 8, posted http://www. tucfa.com/wp-content/uploads/2011/09/CA2011-2013web.pdf.

**p. 136.** "Teacher gets his job back after art college fired him over student beheading a chicken in cafeteria," *National Post,* May 16, 2013, http://news.nationalpost.com/2013/05/16/teacher-gets-his -job-back-after-art-college-fired-him-over-student-beheading-a -chicken-in-cafeteria.

**pp. 138–139.** "A statement from Elizabeth Cannon, President of the University of Calgary, regarding remarks made by Tom Flanagan," February 28, 2013, http://www.ucalgary.ca/news/statements /february2013/flanagan.

**pp. 139–140.** *Employment Equity Act* (SC 1995, c. 44).

**pp. 142–143.** Elizabeth Cannon to Mary-Ellen Tyler, June 5, 2013, attached to email from Sheila Miller to Tom Flanagan, June 10, 2013.

**p. 144.** CAUT letter posted on the SAFS website: http://www.safs.ca /issuescases/CAUT%20to%20Cannon%20re%20Flanagan-1.pdf.

**pp. 145–148.** SAFS letter posted on its website: http://www.safs .ca/issuescases/safslettertocannon.htm.

**p. 148.** "Canada's Leading Anti-Human Trafficking Activist Rebutt's [sic] Tom Flanagan's Child Porn Comments," http://filipinojournal .com/alberta/local-news/news/canada%E2%80%99s-leading -anti-human-trafficking-activist-rebutt%E2%80%99s-tom-flanagan %E2%80%99s-child-porn-comments.html.

**p. 149.** Lukaszuk quoted in James Wood, "Flanagan exiled for porn remark; Professor questions harm of child photos," *Calgary Herald,* March 1, 2013, http://search.proquest.com.ezproxy.lib.ucalgary.ca /docview/1314142512/1402C897D9D5414AB0B/5?accountid=9838.

**p. 149.** Jeff Green, "Flanagan's views called 'repugnant': Seeing child porn shouldn't be a crime, says former adviser," *Toronto Star*, March 1, 2013, http://search.proquest.com.ezproxy.lib.ucalgary.ca/docview/1314788519/1402C8D08A84CBC2D4F/9?accountid=9838.

**p. 152.** Liebling quoted in Noam Cohen, "Surviving without newspapers," *New York Times*, June 6, 2009, http://www.nytimes.com/2009/06/07/weekinreview/07cohen.html?_r=0.

**p. 153.** Bruce Wallace, "Policy Options Editor Responds to National Post on Tom Flanagan Affair," https://www.facebook.com/IRPP.org/posts/497555140280025.

**p. 155.** "Academic Freedom," *New World Encyclopedia*, http://www.newworldencyclopedia.org/entry/Academic_freedom.

**p. 161.** http://www.cbc.ca/thesundayedition/essays/2013/03/17/michael-1/. I couldn't find the comments when I revisited the site August 23, 2013.

**p. 165.** Marvin Olasky, *The Tragedy of American Compassion* (Wheaton, IL: Crossway Books, 1992).

## CHAPTER 7

**pp. 170–173.** Criminal Code (RSC, 1985, c. C-46), s. 163.1, http://laws-lois.justice.gc.ca/eng/acts/C-46.

**p. 174.** *Romeo and Juliet*, Act 1, Scene 3, verse 12.

**p. 174.** http://en.wikipedia.org/wiki/Puberty

**p. 176.** http://www.cbc.ca/news/canada/nova-scotia/story/2013 /08/15/ns-rehtaeh-parsons-accused-appearance.html.

**p. 177.** http://forensicpsychologist.blogspot.ca/2012/12/apa-rejects-hebephilia-last-of-three.html.

**pp. 177–178.** Robert Wright, *The Moral Animal* (New York: Vintage Books, 1994), p. 65.

**p. 179.** http://en.wikipedia.org/wiki/Characters_of_Glee.

**p. 180.** Re Eli Langer, http://www.cbc.ca/news/background/childporn.

**p. 181.** Associated Press, "Child webcam sting nets 54 Canadians," http://www.cbc.ca/m/touch/news/story/1.2355851.

**p. 183.** Re masturbation, http://www.circinfo.org/Circumcision _and_masturbation.html.

**p. 183.** http://en.wikipedia.org/wiki/The_Contest.

**p. 186.** Sexual assault, Criminal Code, ss. 271–273

**pp. 190–192.** Angela W. Eke, Michael C. Seto, and Jeannette Williams, "Examining the Criminal History and Future Offending of Child Pornography Offenders: An Extended Prospective Follow-up Study," *Law and Human Behavior* 35 (2011), pp. 470–471. Quote is from p. 476.

**p. 193.** Adam Walsh Child Protection and Safety Act (2006), Pub. L. 109–248.

**p. 193.** Rachel Aviv, "The Science of Sex Abuse," *The New Yorker,* January 14, 2013, http://www.newyorker.com/reporting/2013 /01/14/130114fa_fact_aviv.

**p. 194.** The report is discussed in Emily Bazelon, "Passive Pedophiles: Are child porn viewers less dangerous than we thought?" *Slate,* April 25, 2013, http://www.slate.com/articles/news_and_politicscrime/2013 /04/child_pornography_viewers_how_dangerous_are_they.html. The report itself is at http://www.ussc.gov/Legislative_and_Public _Affairs/Congressional_Testimony_and_Reports/Sex_Offense_Topics /201212_Federal_Child_Pornography_Offenses/Full_Report_to _Congress.pdf.

**p. 195.** Philip Jenkins, *Beyond Tolerance: Child Pornography on the Internet* (New York: New York University Press, 2003).

## CHAPTER 8

**pp. 200–201.** Aristotle, *Rhetoric,* 1356a.

**pp. 201–204.** Jan Wong, *Out of the Blue: A Memoir of Workplace Depression* (Toronto: Self-published, 2012).

**p. 204.** "Maclean's cover labels Quebec 'most corrupt,'" *Toronto Star,* September 25, 2010, http://www.thestar.com/news/ canada/2010/09/25/macleans_cover_labels_quebec_most_corrupt. html. The issue of *Maclean's* was dated October 4, 2010, but went on sale before that. Charest's letter is reprinted in http://news.national-post.com/2010/09/29/jean-charests-letter-to-macleans/. The House of Commons motion is reprinted in http://www2.macleans. ca/2010/09/29/house-of-commons-censures-macleans. Rogers apology, http://www.cbc.ca/news/canada/montreal/story /2010/09/30/rogers-apologizes-for-bonhomme-cover-page.html.

**p. 206.** Repeal of s. 13, http://news.nationalpost.com/2013/06/27/hate-speech-no-longer-part-of-canadas-human-rights-act/.

**p. 211.** Plato, *Republic,* 2.359a–2.360d.

**pp. 212–213.** Niall Ferguson reported in http://www.fa-mag.com/news/harvard-professor-gay-bashes-keynes-14173.html.

**p. 213, 216–217.** Ferguson letter in http://www.thecrimson.com/article/2013/5/7/Ferguson-Apology-Keynes.

**p. 214.** Keynes quoted in http://www.forbes.com/sites/jerrybowyer/2013/05/12/perhaps-niall-ferguson-had-a-point-about-keynes/2.

**pp. 217–218.** John Cook, "For Sale: A Video of Toronto Mayor Rob Ford Smoking Crack Cocaine," *Gawker,* May 16, 2013, http://gawker.com/for-sale-a-video-of-toronto-mayor-rob-ford-smoking-cra-507736569.

**p. 218.** Robyn Doolittle and Kevin Donovan, "Ford in 'Crack Video' Scandal," *Toronto Star,* May 17, 2013, http://search.proquest.com.ezproxy.lib.ucalgary.ca/docview/1352730298/140692C51164B149F4B/27?accountid=9838.

**p. 218.** "Timeline of Rob Ford Video Scandal," http://en.wikipedia.org/wiki/Timeline_of_Rob_Ford_video_scandal.

**pp. 218–219.** "Rob Ford caught on video in violent rant," *Toronto Star*, November 7, 2013, http://www.thestar.com/news/gta/2013/11/07/mayor_rob_ford_caught_in_video_rant.html.

**pp. 222–224.** Levin's arrest is described in http://news.nationalpost.com/2013/07/08/benjamin-levin-u-of-t-professor-arrested-on-child-pornography-charges.

**p. 223.** Lawrence Martin, "Canada's political scholars fiddle while Rome burns," *Globe and Mail*, June 4, 2013, http://www.theglobeandmail .com/commentary/canadas-political-scholars-fiddle-while-rome-burns /article12319809.

**pp. 224.** Quoted in Michael Kurts, assistant vice-president, Strategic Communications and Marketing, to Tom Flanagan, July 17, 2013, email message.

**pp. 224.** Ezra Levant, https://www.facebook.com/permalink. php?story_fbid=481746671918565&id=131404586952777.

**pp. 224.** Michael Coren, "The Levin factor, *Toronto Sun,* July 17, 2013, http://www.torontosun.com/2013/07/12/the-levin-factor.